I like what you have done with the book. As a matter of fact, I would consider using it as a text for teaching a class in my church on how to manage personal finances.

K. Sterling, EdD., Louisiana

I found this book to be both entertaining and informative. I would recommend it for those who are in financial distress or those who desire to shore up their financial future. It is written for all to understand and the author appears to truly believe in the strategies he has recommended. Excellent book for you couples embarking on careers that seek financial fitness.

J. McManis, Louisiana

This is without doubt one of the greatest books ever written about personal finance. I learned so much in a short period of time. The steps were simple and easy to follow. I can't wait to get started on my own financial fitness.

A. Hartong, Louisiana

I never knew that taking control of my money could be so simple. Just with a couple of the ideas in this book I have found several ways to build wealth and reduce liabilities in my own personal financial situation. This book is definitely a must for anyone interested in being debt-free.

T. Hughes, Alabama

Before I read Financial Fitness I was working nearly 300 days per year away from home just to keep my head above water. Still I was about to be sued by a credit card company and I was seriously considering Bankruptcy. Over the past few years Financial Fitness has been the tool I used to regain control of my personal finances. Now I have no credit card debt at all. I have a house note that I pay extra on every month and my utilities.That's it! Thanks to the things I learned in this book I now work a regular 28 and 14 day schedule without having to work over just to pay my bills.

J. Verdin, Towboat Captain, Louisiana

FINANCIAL FITNESS

THE INSTRUCTION BOOK
FOR YOUR PAYCHECK

BY JOE KENT

Note for Librarians: A cataloguing record for this book is available from Library
and Archives Canada at www.collectionscanada.ca/amicus/index-e.html

Printed in Victoria, BC, Canada.

ISBN: 978-1-4269-0144-7 (sc)
ISBN: 978-1-4269-0146-1 (e-book)

We at Trafford believe that it is the responsibility of us all, as both individuals and corporations, to make choices that are environmentally and socially sound. You, in turn, are supporting this responsible conduct each time you purchase a Trafford book, or make use of our publishing services. To find out how you are helping, please visit www.trafford.com/responsiblepublishing.html

Our mission is to efficiently provide the world's finest, most comprehensive book publishing service, enabling every author to experience success. To find out how to publish your book, your way, and have it available worldwide, visit us online at www.trafford.com

Trafford rev. 6/23/2009

Trafford
PUBLISHING® www.trafford.com

North America & international
toll-free: 1 888 232 4444 (USA & Canada)
phone: 250 383 6864 ♦ fax: 250 383 6804 ♦ email: info@trafford.com

The United Kingdom & Europe
phone: +44 (0)1865 487 395 ♦ local rate: 0845 230 9601
facsimile: +44 (0)1865 481 507 ♦ email: info.uk@trafford.com

Contents

About the author
Acknowledgments
Introduction
Disclaimer Notice

PART 1
WHAT YOU DON'T KNOW CAN HURT YOU 17
THE EDUCATION PROCESS

CHAPTER 1
THE DEBT
TRAP...18
-THE PROBLEM-THE SOLUTION

CHAPTER 2
NO MORE SMOKE AND MIRRORS...24
-THE NUMBER 72-THE NUMBER 72 REVIEW

CHAPTER 3
AVOIDING THE QUARTER OF A MILLION-DOLLAR MISTAKE...........30
-WHAT IS A MUTUAL FUND-DIVERSIFICATION-HOW TO INVEST-DOLLAR COST
AVERAGING-401K THE SMART INVESTMENT-MAKING MONEY IN A MUTUAL FUND

CHAPTER 4
THE NINE-LETTER DIRTY WORD...40
-CASH VALUE LIFE INSURANCE-UNIVERSAL LIFE INSURANCE AND "PAID UP
POLICIES"-POLICIES THAT PAY DIVIDENDS-TERM LIFE INSURANCE-BUY TERM AND
INVEST THE DIFFERENCE-BUT UNCLE ROB IS MY AGENT-BUY TERM AND INVEST
THE DIFFERENCE RULES-RAISE YOUR DEDUCTIBLES

CHAPTER 5
A LITTLE LAGNIAPPE...54
-ASK FOR A LOWER INTEREST RATE-THE DEBT ELIMINATOR-RE-POSITION YOUR
ASSETS-KNOW YOUR MORTGAGE-THE LOWEST POSSIBLE FIXED RATE-RETAIN A
LAWYER-A 30 YEAR MORTGAGE?-THE MORTGAGE ACCELERATOR-THE NINE-
LETTER DIRTY WORD RE-VISITED-UNCLE SAM IS NOT SANTA CLAUSE-CLEAR THE
SMOKE-

CHAPTER 6
ACCELERATE YOUR INCOME...67
-$100 EXTRA PER MONTH-EXPLORE YOUR TALENTS-GET RICH QUICK

CHAPTER 7
BANKING ON FINANCIAL FITNESS...74
-BANKRUPTCY?-CREDIT COUNSELORS?-CHECK YOUR CREDIT REPORT-THE
CREDIT STIMULATOR

CHAPTER 8

RE-INVENTING THE WHEEL..84
-THE WISH LIST-CATEGORIZE EACH WISH-PICK THE FIVE MOST IMPORTANT
WISHES-CREATE A JOURNAL-CREATE A DEFINITE PLAN OF ACTION

PART II

SCHOOL IS OUT, GO TO WORK!..93
THE OFFICIAL INSTRUCTIONS FOR YOUR PAYCHECK

CHAPTER 9

YOUR WISH IS MY COMMAND...**95**
-THE MISSION STATEMENT-FIND OUT WHERE YOU ARE-PREPARE A FINANCIAL STATEMENT-
TRACK YOUR SPENDING-CREATE A BUDGET-BALANCE YOUR CHECKING ACCOUNT

FINANCIAL FITNESS PLANS OF ACTION: #1 OBTAIN A VIVID PICTURE OF WHERE YOU
ARE-#2 AVOID THE QUARTER OF A MILLION-DOLLAR MISTAKE-#3 OPERATE ON A CASH ONLY
BASIS-#4 THE CREDIT STIMULATOR-#5 RE-POSITION YOUR ASSETS-#6 ELIMINATE DEBT

CHAPTER 10

FROM FITNESS TO INDEPENDENCE...122
-GED-SPECIALIZED TRAINING-BUILD AN EMERGENCY FUND-DETERMINE
RETIREMENT AMOUNT-PLAN YOUR RETIREMENT NOW-LIVE ON 70% OF YOUR
INCOME-THE OTHER 30%-FINANCIAL INDEPENDENCE PLAN OF ACTION

About The Author

Content in the belief that if you search then you will find, **Joe Kent** has been searching for financial fitness since an early age. Raised up in rural Georgia by a middle-income family, Joe quickly learned the value of a dollar. Although his family was not destitute and Joe rarely wanted for anything, they certainly were not rich. At the age of 14 the industrious young man began to work summers as a brick mason's helper in order to afford the extra things that he knew his family could not get for him.

In studying his surroundings Joe found that most of the people he knew lived from paycheck to paycheck and only a few were fortunate enough to be wealthy. Soon the imaginative dreamer started to ponder the idea of finding a better way of living besides the old 9 to 5 job and living out the "American Dream".

By the age of 16, Joe had bought into and investigated several get-rich-quick-schemes only to find that they were just that, "schemes". Still he knew that if he did the same things and took the same jobs as most of the people he knew, then he would end up in the same financial situation that they were in. Yet Joe out of frustration and necessity did follow in the very footsteps that he had tried so hard to avoid.

The burning fire of his dreams died down to just an ember; still he lay awake at night, thinking, hoping, and believing that there was something else for him in life. Finally at the age of 19 good fortune came Joe's way when a friend introduced him to a financial services company.

The ideas presented were in fact secrets that mostly only rich people knew and practiced. Those ideas made a lot of sense to Joe and they served to re-awaken the dreamer and fan the fires of his desires.

It was with great excitement that Joe began to work part-time with that company and started a career educating common people like himself about personal finance. Joe continued to learn everything he could while in the financial services industry. He obtained an insurance license as well as a securities license and worked his way up to District Leader in that company. A position that was just two positions away from the coveted Regional Vice-President position.

Joe very much enjoyed helping people get their financial houses in order, however his first love had been writing; specifically country song writing. Joe Kent wrote his first song in the middle of a night when he could not sleep about the time he was 7 years old. At present he has over 300 songs to his credit with copyrights and 23 of those produced and recorded on demos.

In 1996 Joe made a career change to towboats and moved to Louisiana. The towboat industry offered a 28 days on and 14 days off schedule. Starting out as a deckhand he reasoned that he could use the days off to shop his demos around Nashville. That is a dream that he still actively pursues. Because of his work ethic Joe quickly worked his way up the chain of command on the boats. Soon he was a 2nd mate and then worked his way up to 1st mate.

Joe eventually obtained his license with the United States Coast Guard and is now a pilot on the boats. Joe still enjoys helping people when it comes to personal finance and is frequently asked his advice by his friends, family and sometimes co-workers concerning their 401K and other money matters.

With juggling his towboat career and a potential song writing career Joe has been unable to return to the financial services industry as he one day hopes to do. So as a result of song writing writer's block Joe put his writing energy into a book.

FINANCIAL FITNESS contains those ideas that he first learned about when he was 19 as well as a lot of other ideas that Joe has found as a result of research and personal experience. By reducing these ideas to paper Joe knew he could reach a wider audience than if he were doing it one on one.

Commenting on his book FINANCIAL FITNESS Joe said, "I love to write and I love to help people, so FINANCIAL FITNESS was a labor of love for me. Not only that but it got my creative juices flowing once again and I now have several new ideas for songs as well as several ideas for books."

Keep your eyes open for more books by this author, if they prove to be as beneficial as this one then it will be well worth the investment. Also listen to your radio and maybe someday you will hear one of Joe's songs.
 In the meantime Joe will continue to write and create because that is his destiny.

Acknowledgments

To my precious and loving wife Denise, for your love, patience and devotion. You have stood by me even through times when you had no reason to stand by me. There have been struggles but you have been as faithful as the day is long on the longest day of the year. You have encouraged me, helped me and have been a great source of inspiration. A lot of great songs have been written as a direct result of our relationship, and I love and admire you.

To Dianna Jean and Jessica Michelle, for keeping the faith. Never have I spent a day without you on my mind. I am with you in mind and heart when I can't be there in body. Some day **ALL** of your dreams will come true. You are my heart.

To mom and dad, for your undying faith in my abilities and me. You believed in me when I didn't even believe in myself. Thanks for your support and your help.

Introduction

We live in a world where everything comes with instructions. The bicycle that you bought for your children's Christmas all the way down to the shampoo you buy all have instructions. The one thing that does not come with instructions that should, is something that you get every week or every other week. Your paycheck.

Hi, my name is Joe Kent and I have virtually no consumer debt. The only credit cards I own usually get paid in full every month. I do not live from paycheck to paycheck and I have money left over at the end of the month to invest for my future.

I am not making that statement in order to try to look superior or prove that I am smarter or more talented than any one of you. I am not a CPA nor am I some "Big Wheel" Fortune 500 executive. I am a common person just like many of you. So what gives me the right to author a book on personal finance? Mainly experience gives me the right.

You see I went through a divorce, I filed for bankruptcy twice, and I lost a home to foreclosure. So my previous statement did not come without heartache, and disappointment along the way.

I have however learned a lot about personal finance and how to apply it in order to get out of debt. I have done research, I have talked to and learned from a lot of people who were financially successful I have studied at the school of "hard knocks".

I once had dinner with a group of people at the Ritz in which the lowest earner at the table made over $100,000 per year and the top earner was making over $2,000,000 per year and the subject of the conversation at dinner was how they accomplish goals. On another particular occasion, I got off a Greyhound bus on the opposite side of the same town and bought a few beers for the homeless that were gathered on a loading dock. I heard their stories of heartache and misery and the reasons some of those people were there.

I have seen the worst as well as the best that humanity has to offer and I have learned from both. Although my experience does not make me an expert it certainly has given me some powerful insights that I would like to share.

There were two things that brought me to the financial position that I currently enjoy. Number one was a proper education in how money works and how to get it working for me instead of against me. This I learned at an early age and yet I still had financial difficulties.
I was very frustrated because I had the knowledge and had met literally hundreds of people who had applied the very same techniques and succeeded.

Therefore secondly I had to learn some direction and discipline in order to apply the education that I had learned. That unfortunately I had to learn the hard way. I hope to teach you the best of what I have learned in my education process and also give you the direction to develop the discipline that you will need in order to avoid many of the set-backs that I have experienced over the years.

Remember the old saying "If I only knew then what I know now"? Well, if I could only go back ten years ago and give my younger self a copy of this book maybe I could have avoided a lot of the mistakes I made. Fortunately you will be able to learn from my education as well as my experience and hopefully your road to financial fitness will be a little less bumpy than mine was.

Most people are plagued with consumer debt. They owe banks, credit card companies, finance companies, even friends and relatives.

Those debts can follow people all their lives and by the time they make it to retirement they end up retiring broke and have to spend their last days struggling to make ends meet.

I'm sure you know people in that situation. I'm here to say that there is a debt problem in this country and it can be corrected if you have the right information and the discipline to change.

People in general do not plan on failing financially, why that would be absurd; they were just not giving good information in order to make the proper decision. The problem is that most people are never properly educated on how to make their money work for them instead of against them.

The ideas and principles that will be discussed in this writing are not taught in school as a matter of a fact there are people and institution that hope you never learn what will be discussed here. The reason the secrets are kept secret is that if your money is not making you rich then it is making someone else rich.

You've heard that you have got to have money to make money. Well that's true to a certain extent, but do you realize at even $6.00 an hour if you worked from the time you were eighteen until you were sixty-five that you would make almost $600,000 in your life time.

With the proper tools, a little time and patience even on a meager income you can become financially fit, and possibly financially independent. It does not matter how much you make, what matters is how much you keep.

I am about to attempt to show you how to keep more of what you make and live a more productive and prosperous life. It is not my intention to teach you how to become a miser. If you are a miser then you are only one letter away from misery. The happiest most well adjusted people I have met have been frugal yet benevolent. Yes, you should develop your assets and reduce your liabilities but you should also be charitable to the people less fortunate than yourself.

One final note and a word of caution before we begin, I do not have all the answers, but I do have some ideas that will help you along your journey to financial fitness. Edit these ideas all you wish, you certainly do not have to take my word for everything.

If something makes sense use it, if it does not make sense then discard it. I do however, challenge you to ask yourself this question. If you have the same amount of hours in a day and the same opportunity as a self made rich man does, then why are you struggling still living from paycheck to paycheck.

Could it be that no one has ever giving you instructions on how to use your paycheck?

There is however a word of caution. There will be things in this book that will excite and motivate you and you will want to rush out and get started right away. This set of instructions should be used like any other instructions. Do not start the project until you have read the entire book.

Patience is a virtue and it is a must when dealing with your financial fitness. Some of these ideas will take months or even years to accomplish depending on your particular situation. So take the time to read and study these ideas before you begin.

Here now is the instruction book for your paycheck. If it only helps one family reach financial fitness instead of disaster and gives them peace instead of turmoil then I will consider this project a complete success.

Disclaimer Notice

Further more you should expect to invest a lot of time, and consistent effort in your pursuit. Years may be required in order to produce the desired effect.

Every effort has been made to produce an instruction book that is both accurate as well as complete.

However there may be mistakes in content as well as typographical errors. Therefore you should use this manual as a general guide and not as your only source of information.

Again, FINANCIAL FITNESS was created to educate and entertain. No one involved in the creation or distribution of this text shall be held liable or responsible to any person or entity for any loss or damages caused, or alleged to have been caused, directly or indirectly, by any information contained in this book.

If you do not wish to be bound by the above notice, please return this book promptly for a full refund. If this book is not returned within ten days of receipt of purchase it will be assumed that the above notice is agreed to.

WHAT YOU DON'T KNOW CAN HURT YOU!

THE EDUCATION PROCESS

CHAPTER 1
THE DEBT TRAP

Money is a medium that replaced the old "barter system" in which you would trade your goods and services for other goods and services that you needed but did not have. It is now a standard for measuring how much something is worth.

Your time spent away from your family while you are working is measured in so many dollars per hour or per day. Your time is not actually what your employer is paying for but the value that you put into those hours or days. You have to create value in order to earn money and the more valuable you are the more money you will make.

With that money you can then purchase the goods and services that everyone wants to supply for their family. Everyone has the basic responsibility of providing the necessities if they wish to raise a family.

Things such as food, shelter and clothing are a must and these have to be provided for first. Next we have to provide for insurance on our homes, our health, our vehicles and even our lives in order to protect our families from financial loss should something happen.

Along with our insurance needs most people would like to have an emergency fund in order to further protect our families from loss.

Being that we are humans we not only have needs but we have wants such as a vacation, a new car and all the gadgets and toys that modern technology has brought to our economy.

At some point we have to consider providing for our children's education and then eventually for retirement.

THE PROBLEM

With everything that we have out there to spend money on it is a bit overwhelming to decide what we should purchase and what is really too expensive.

Unfortunately, banks, finance and credit card companies have solved this problem for us. At one time when you ran out of money and had a zero balance you could no longer purchase anything. It's not that way any more. Now you can have whatever you want today with little or no money down and easy terms. The minimum payment is not that much. Hey, just think about it, $30 per month is only $1 per day. Anyone can afford that.

Welcome to the debt trap or should I say the death trap. The reason I say the death trap is because with all of those minimum monthly payments that we are offered you no longer have to stop at a zero balance, you can now go right past zero at $50, $100 or more per month at a time. Eventually you have more debt than you have money to pay.

Have you ever heard the saying "I have too much month left over at the end of the money"? This cycle will kill you financially, emotionally, and spiritually. It is a death trap that will murder your quality of life. It has caused depression, divorces and suicides.

Everytime that you are asked to pay for something on credit that person is essentially saying that you will work so many hours per week for them. You may feel that debt is your only way to obtain the things you want and need, but at the end of the month when you are broke and unhappy and the creditors are calling, is it really worth it?

Too much debt is a break down in the moral fiber of this country yet nearly every commercial you see on TV is offering something that you can purchase on your credit card or make no payments until next year.

Then the majority of the rest of the commercials are lawyers that will help you file for bankruptcy or credit counseling services to help you get out of the debt you are in. That tells me that there is a problem that needs to be addressed. So what are we going to do about it?

THE SOLUTION

Before I give you the solution to debt lets put a few things in perspective.

NUMBER ONE: Your current financial position does not define you as a human being. Just because you owe a lot of money and find it hard to meet your obligations does not make you a bad person. It is embarrassing at times, believe me I know, I've been there. That in no way however reflects on your character.

NUMBER TWO: Money is not the root of all evil. The bible says that the **love** of money is the root of all evil. Do not sabotage yourself because you do not believe that you deserve any better than you have right now. You have just as much a right to accumulate wealth and live a prosperous life as anyone else. Money is not the love of your life nor is money everything. Be sure to work on yourself spiritually, emotionally, and physically as well as financially.

NUMBER THREE: No one has the right to kill you because you owe them money. There are no debtor's prisons. You may get sued and you may have hardships while you are working your plans toward financial fitness but for the most part you are okay. Just do not give up and have a little peace in the fact that this is not the end of the world. You are not going to die because you are in debt.

NUMBER FOUR: Things are never as good or as bad as they seem. Although I have accomplished a lot working towards financial fitness, it could still be better. I could be financially independent. Of course it could be worse, I could be broke and living under a bridge. No matter where you are at financially you can always find someone that is worse off than yourself. Take comfort in the fact that you are not the Lone Ranger no matter how far away from your goals you may be.

NUMBER FIVE: Misery loves company so keep your plans toward financial fitness to yourself. If you tell friends and family what you are doing then you will probably hear a lot of reasons why this will not work for you. Even people that care about you will sometimes discourage you.

If you would like to recommend this book to others then that is fine but keep your personal finances personal.

NUMBER SIX: Do not procrastinate and never give up until you have accomplished financial fitness. Some techniques in this book will take some time and you will have disappointments and setbacks. You will however never accomplish what you do not try.

Most people work harder for their employers than they do for themselves. Do a good job at work like you should but work at least that hard at designing your life.

If you are content in the fact that you are working towards financial fitness then you will have a sense of pride and relief that will be reflected in your personal life as well as at your job. You will in fact find that you are more confident to handle the little difficulties that life will throw your way.

Now back to the subject at hand, the solution. The solution to your financial troubles is in a way very simple. You have to get **MAD**.

MONEY
AGAINST
DEBT

Eventually you have to get sick and tired of being in debt to the point that it offends you to be offered anything on credit. If you are not totally tired of the position that you are in then there's no technique that will help you because you have to have the commitment to work it and follow through.

You will learn in the pages of this book how to use your money against debt but you will also have to commit to not getting in debt again. The only solution to a debt problem is to quit accumulating debt and to pay off what you already owe.

Wow that is a mouth full and to most of you may seem impossible, but I am not just saying this I will show you how to accomplish it. For now see it for what it is, the solution in its simplest form. The solution is really that simple but it's not easy.

You will have to find out where you are financially, decide where you want to go and develop plans that will help you arrive. It is my job in the pages that follow to help you get **MAD** and use your money against debt until you have accomplished financial fitness.

If you take what you are about to learn and apply it eventually you will be completely debt-free and will avoid the debt (death) trap altogether.

Imagine having no more credit card debts or anymore bank notes and being able to enjoy the money you earn. It will greatly improve your quality of life and your whole attitude will change. The sooner you get started the better so let's move on to chapter 2, NO MORE SMOKE AND MIRRORS, and begin the education process.

T.J. KENT MUSIC

I'M SO BROKE
WRITTEN BY T.J. KENT

Well, I went on down to my P.O. box
  I opened it up and guess what I got
A big stack of bills that I know I can't pay
  No matter how I try there's just no way
Threw them on the pile that I keep in the kitchen
  'Cause I'm so broke I can't even pay attention

Chorus:
I'm so broke I can't even pay attention
  Someone should put me on some kind of pension
If there's a way I'd sure like to learn it
  But you can't get blood out of a turnip
Hey just in case I forgot to mention
  I'm so broke I can't even pay attention

Now I need some kind of financial hero
  'Cause they done let me go way past zero
I owe everyone including their brother
  I even got a loan from my mother
So put it on my account will you please honey
  On account of I ain't got no money
In my wallet there's a big ole' indention
  'Cause I'm so broke I can't even pay attention

Repeat Chorus

Ending:
My head is full of all kinds of tension
  'Cause I'm so broke I can't even pay attention

© 1995 T.J. Kent music
Member BMI

CHAPTER 2
NO MORE SMOKE AND MIRRORS

It is pretty obvious that most people do not understand how to get money working properly for them. We live in one of the richest countries in the world yet most of the people that retire every year do so on an income that is considered to be at the poverty level. The main reason for this problem is a lack of financial education. Their money is working for someone else instead of working for them. This coupled with the fact that most people have high interest debts and it's plain to see why financial failure is so common. People are not given instructions with their paycheck.

As a matter of a fact there are a lot of smoke and mirrors out there to make sure they never learn how to get their money working for them instead of against them. The reason why there are smoke and mirrors is simple. If your money is not making you wealthy then it is making someone else wealthy. Also if you learn to take control of your finances and become debt-free then you are no longer paying all those high interest rates every month.

Therefore the people you are paying every month do not want you to know what you are about to learn. Without attacking any institution or organization personally I will deal with just the facts and you decide who it is that put up the smoke and mirrors.

THE NUMBER 72

Seventy-two is just a number and without the information contained in this chapter would really not be any more unique than any other number.

Seventy-two became very significant to me however about the time that I was in the third grade. Little did I know that it would mean the world to me once I grew up and learned how to apply it to personal finance.

When I was in the third grade we were learning our multiplication tables and were expected to know them by heart. I always did well in school but in the third grade I was having trouble memorizing the answers at the drop of a hat. I could come up with the answers just fine but it took me a little time. My dad was determined that I would learn my multiplication tables and would be able to give the answers immediately and without hesitation.

I on the other hand just could not remember them that well, yet I could sing virtually every rock and country song that played on the radio without missing a word. I don't know why I didn't think to make up a multiplication song and put a beat to it so that I could memorize all those numbers, but I guess at that age the songwriter in me hadn't come out yet.

Anyway my dad was a Vietnam vet and unquestionably the drill sergeant that ruled our home. That is in no way a derogatory comment towards my dad, my point is that I was raised up strict. In my dad's mind, if I knew all the words to all those songs then I could and would learn my multiplication tables or I would have to face the music so to speak.

The more he tried the more frustrated he became because I just could not rattle off the answers the way he expected. Finally one day my dad asked me what nine times eight was. It took me a few minutes of counting on my fingers but I finally gave the correct answer of seventy-two.

My dad said that I was correct and from that day forward any time that he asked me what nine times eight was that I had better be able to provide the answer without hesitation, seventy-two. For a couple of days straight my dad at random would ask me what nine times eight was and I without hesitation would answer seventy-two.

Eventually I did learn my multiplication tables or at least I faked it enough until I got to the point in school where we were allowed to use calculators. Thank God for calculators! Nevertheless I will never ever have to think about what nine times eight is. My dad will even now on occasions when we are talking say, "By the way what's nine times eight?" and after we have a laugh I will respond "seventy-two".

Now, I am sure you are wondering what that has to do with the subject matter of this book? Well, the story doesn't have anything to do with it but the number seventy-two certainly does.

In order for you to make money work properly for you, it is critical to understand how to apply the number seventy-two to your personal finances.

Basically the number seventy-two tells you how often your money will double at a given interest rate. For example if you took $1,000 down to the bank and started an account and let's say they agreed to give you a 3% return for the use of your money. 72 divided by 3 equals 24. That means that your $1,000 would double every 24 years.

One time investment of $1,000

	3%	6%	12%
6 years			
12 years			
18 years			
24 years	$2,000		
30 years			
36 years			
42 years			
48 years	$4,000		

Now if you could get a 6% return on your money maybe in a certificate of deposit that would mean twice the interest so you would have twice the money in the same amount of time, right? Wrong! You see 72 divided by 6 equals 12 which means that your money will double every 12 years.

You would have $16,000 in the same amount of time that it took you to accumulate $4,000, because of the effect of compound interest.

One time investment of $1,000

	3%	6%	12%
6 years			
12 years		$2,000	
18 years			
24 years	$2,000	$4,000	
30 years			
36 years		$8,000	
42 years			
48 years	$4,000	$16,000	

Now in order to get a 12% return on your money, you have to invest your money to do that and there are conservative investments out there that have a track record of 12% and better.

At this point I don't want you to focus on where you will get a 12% return on your money. That will be discussed in chapter 3. For now just apply the number seventy-two and look at the awesome amount of difference that there is between saving your money and investing your money.

Ask yourself, do most Americans if they do either one, do they invest their money or do they save it?

Most Americans have a hard time coming up with the money to do either one but if you said "save" then you are absolutely right. Most people do not know how to invest their money because they have not been taught. Furthermore there are smoke and mirrors in place to discourage common people from investing. One being a guarantee.

Now keep in mind that there are plenty of conservative investments out there that you can get a 12% return and better on your money. There are however no guarantees when investing your money, but let's take a look at what the cost of a guarantee may be. 72 divided by 12 equals 6 which as you have already learned means that your $1,000 will double every 6 years.

One time investment of $1,000

	3%	6%	12%
6 years			$2,000
12 years		$2,000	$4,000
18 years			$8,000
24 years	$2,000	$4,000	$16,000
30 years			$32,000
36 years		$8,000	$64,000
42 years			$128,000
48 years	$4,000	$16,000	$256,000

   As you know financial institutions do not take your money and put it in a box with your name on it. They use your money; in other words they invest it and they pay you interest for using it.

   Of course in today's economy you will not be getting a 3% return but if you did you would have $4000 at the end of 48 years with a one-time investment of $1000. The financial institution that you loaned your $1000 to accumulated $256,000 minus the $4000 they owe you. They cleared $252,000 and you made $3,000.

   As you can see by saving instead of investing people are potentially making a quarter of a million-dollar mistake in their financial future.
   No wonder financial institutions have the biggest buildings in town with marble floors and we have linoleum. Someone else is investing your money and the profits are paying for those marble floors and it's due in part to not being able to see through the smoke and mirrors.

   Now don't get me wrong these institutions have their uses, which will be discussed in a later chapter but for now see them as they really are with no smoke and mirrors. When you put your money in they pay you for its use but they invest it and keep the profit. They do the same thing with your money that you could be doing for yourself and they don't want you to know.

   In other words you can by-pass those institutions and invest your money in the same places they do and keep the profit for yourself.
   Of course that $1000 you saved was guaranteed but at what cost; a quarter of a million dollars maybe?

Your money is already being invested; the question is who is benefiting from it. Now that I have your attention let's move on to how you can invest for yourself in chapter three, AVOIDING THE QUARTER OF A MILLION-DOLLAR MISTAKE.

THE NUMBER 72 REVIEW

Take the interest rate that you can get on your money and divide it into the number 72 and the answer equals the number of years that it will take for your money to double.

72 DIVIDED BY 3(%) EQUALS 24 YEARS
72 DIVIDED BY 6(%) EQUALS 12 YEARS
72 DIVIDED BY 12(%) EQUALS 6 YEARS

CHAPTER 3
AVOIDING THE QUARTER OF A MILLION-DOLLAR MISTAKE

Everyone knows that when you take your money down to a financial institution such as the bank that they don't just put it in a box with your name on it. They pay you for the use of your money and they invest it.

Part of the money you get back in the form of home mortgages car loans and credit cards. Which they usually charge you around 6-11% for a mortgage depending on your credit, the bank, and the prime interest rate. On the credit cards they usually charge you between 18 and 21%. Wow, figure that with The Number 72.

On a larger scale the bank takes your money to professional managers and they invest it in the economy in what is known as common stock.
You can pick up a copy of the bank's annual report to find out how much of their assets are put where. Again this is your money that they agreed to pay you whatever interest rate for its use. Your money is being invested, just not by you.

You have access to the same professional money managers as the bank does through what is known as a mutual fund.

WHAT IS A MUTUAL FUND?

Basically a mutual fund is a company that is in business to invest other people's money in order to make a profit both for the company and the investor. They take my money, your money and hundreds of thousands of other people's money and pool it together and purchase common stock and manage the money for us.

The advantage of this mutual pooling of money is the opportunity to own and share in the profits of companies that would not be available to you as a small investor. For example if you invested in a fund that owned 100,000 shares of AT&T then you would be reaping the benefits of the ownership of those shares without having to spend a small fortune to purchase those shares on your own. For most small investors to purchase those shares would be impossible.

The banks biggest selling point for the reason that you should save your money with them instead of investing on your own is the guarantee. You know the old FDIC, insured up to $100,000. You have already seen what that will cost you. So why would you want to invest your money with no guarantee and risk losing it? The answer is simple, diversification.

DIVERSIFICATION

Safety comes with diversification. Although diversification is not a guarantee it does help to reduce risk. In other words a mutual fund company may spread out your money in over 50 different industries and maybe150 different companies.

Companies such as IBM, Coca-Cola, and Wal* Mart just to name a few may be included in a fund's portfolio. So even though there are no guarantees that you will not lose your money, the chances of all those companies going broke at once is slim to none.

How would you feel about the safety of your money being invested in the type of companies that I just mentioned? That is pretty much the who's who of the American economy and in most people's opinions they are good investments.

Even if the economy did get so bad that all those companies went broke and you had your money in the bank and had the guarantee. What would your money be worth? If there were no economy then your money would just be worthless paper.

When choosing a mutual fund you will receive a prospectus from someone that is licensed by the Security Exchange Commission. Inside the prospectus it will list all the companies that your money will be spread out over. That way you can choose the mutual fund that has the companies that you feel comfortable in investing in. Also you will be guided through on what level of risk you are willing to take in order to achieve your financial goals.

The function of diversification of a mutual fund is that only a small percentage of your money is in any one certain company. To use an old cliché, you do not have all your eggs in one basket, and if one of those companies has a bad year it does not effect you that much overall.

When you own a share of a mutual fund you own a small piece of every one of the companies that is in that particular fund's portfolio.
The significance of diversification is that you can not loose all your money at once like you would were you only investing in one particular company's stock and that company went broke. In other words you have safety in numbers. With diversification comes safety, not a guarantee, but remember that the price of a guarantee is the quarter of a million-dollar mistake.

The question you have to ask yourself when considering a particular fund is how do you feel about the safety of the companies in the portfolio.
However, it really does not matter how you feel about the safety of your money being invested in those companies, because it is already there. What matters is how it gets there and who benefits from it, you or the bank.

When it comes to deciding if you want to invest or not you will want to know a couple of things, if your money will be there if you need it and how much will they pay you on it.
If you do want your money a mutual fund company will have it to you within seven business days.

A mutual fund however is not meant to be a "put and take account" or an emergency account. The purpose of a mutual fund is for long-term investing such as for retirement or a college education for your children.

The basic rule is that if you are not planning on leaving the money in for at least five years, then do not invest it in a mutual fund.

As far as the question of how much will they pay you on your money, in the prospectus that you will receive, you will find a track record of how well that fund has actually done in the past. If the fund continues to do as well in the future then you will have an idea of what to expect. 12% is not just a magic number that I came up with, 12% is considered to be conservative for people that are seeking growth in their investment goals. Each fund varies and the percentage rate is an average, some years may be better than others.

If you were so inclined to you can keep up with how much a fund is worth on a daily basis. All you have to do is go to the financial section of your newspaper. Look up your fund in the list and multiply the shares you own by the share price of that day and you will know how much your fund is worth.

HOW TO INVEST

There are three ways to invest in mutual funds. First is a **lump sum investment** in which you would put in a large sum of money. Maybe you are able to invest $10,000 or $100,000 at one time.

The second way is a **voluntary investment** in which you might put in $500 or $1,000 to open the account and then add to it whenever you like.

The third way and by far the best way is a **systematic investment** in which you put a regular, specified amount in every month. The reason that the systematic investment is better is because you take advantage of the rise and dips in the economy.

DOLLAR COST AVERAGING

For example if you were investing in a fund for $100 every month and the share price was $1 per share then your $100 bought 100 shares.

Now lets say that the second month the share price went down to $.50 per share. The 100 shares you bought are now only worth $50.

Most people would be worried that they are losing money because the share price went down and would want to count their losses and sell out, right?

The good thing is that in the second month your $100 bought twice as many shares, 200 to be exact. Now lets assume that the third month it was still down to $.50 per share and you purchased another 200 shares and then the fourth month it went back up to $1 per share. You bought 400 shares in the second and third month for $.50 per share and now they are worth $1 per share again. You have made money with what experts call dollar cost averaging.

Dollar cost averaging is basically making more money average wise in a fluctuating economy than you would in a steadily rising economy by buying more shares during the dips in the economy.

Lately as of this writing the economy has been down. It is a buyer's market, or a good time to accumulate shares at a low price. Most people think that when the market is down that it is not a good time to invest when actually the opposite is true.

With all the fluctuation especially with consumer confidence being so low lately most people that have never invested before will be understandably reluctant in investing in mutual funds.

Investing is a personal decision that you will have to make on your own but let me remind you that your money is already being invested.
Someone is already buying shares at a low price with your money and when the economy goes back up they will reap the profits.

You might ask how I can be so confident that the economy will come back up. No, I don't have a crystal ball that tells the future but history does repeat itself and the economy has always recovered. But what if history repeats itself and we experience another depression? If that is the case and you are saving your money at the bank with the FDIC insurance how much will it be worth.

I do not wish to spend valuable time here trying to further convince you that investing is right for you because there is still a lot more ground to cover. You weigh the facts and you decide if investing is an option.

If you do decide to invest then you will constantly see the rise and dips but do not panic. Through a systematic investment you will be taking advantage of dollar cost averaging.

October 19, 1987 was named Black Monday because the Dow-Jones Industrial Average fell more than 500 points. This was considered a crash of the economy but the week following Black Monday the crisis had eased off and by the end of 1987 the averages were ahead of the totals at the end of 1986. For the systematic investor that was a time to accumulate a lot more shares for the same amount of money worth even more at the end of 1987.

If you notice the Dow Jones on the news every night they show it going up and down from day to day. The Dow Jones started in 1934 at 60 and it went well over 10,000 a few years ago and now it is lingering around 8,000.

There are 30 companies' stock that make the Dow go up and down and it is like a roller coaster but steadily over the years it has went up. Right now it is down but has started to come back up.

So be prepared for the dips as a matter of a fact if you are investing systematically then you will enjoy seeing them come because of the effect of dollar cost averaging.

401K –THE $MART INVESTMENT

While we are on the subject of systematic investing a good place to start your investment program may be where you work. A lot of companies now offer a 401k plan or a similar Individual Retirement Account (IRA) and most even match what the employee contributes to a certain percentage, usually between 3-20% depending on the company.

There are several advantages to a payroll deduction into a 401k plan. First is the employers match. It is a head start on your money before it even has a chance to start working for you. Whatever percentage the employer matches is like getting that much interest from the start. On the lower percentage side they may match 3% of your salary and on the higher side it may be 20% of what you contribute, either way it is to your advantage.

The second advantage to payroll deduction is that in most cases your contribution is taken out before taxes which means that you can invest up to 10% of your pay and see very little change in your bring home pay.

By doing this you are also paying yourself first before you pay anyone else including Uncle Sam.

The third advantage is that not only is the money tax deferred until you retire and begin to use it. Your 401k plan is also tax deductible, which means you save money at tax time, as long as you do not take it out before a certain age which is usually 59 1/2. A little later we will explore some creative ways to free up some money but right now just by starting an IRA you can reduce your tax burden.

That means that you no longer owe Uncle Sam as much and you can use that money towards your financial fitness plans. This is a **$MART** investment because you are **$**aving **M**oney **A**nd **R**educing **T**axes. Please do however check with your tax advisor on the deductions.

A word of caution when investing in a company sponsored IRA or even an IRA at a bank; they also offer these plans with guaranteed funds that pay low interest. The quarter of a million- dollar mistake is the guarantee. Make sure that if you are seeking growth that you choose a fund that produces growth not guarantees.

The fourth advantage to investing in your 401k plan is that sometimes you have the option of using it as an emergency account. You can actually borrow your money and the interest that you pay goes back into your account. You are paying yourself interest to use your own money.
However keep in mind that when you borrow from your account that you are taking the money out of the market and that amount will only produce the percentage of interest that you are paying on it.

MAKING MONEY IN A MUTUAL FUND

Another distinct advantage to investing in mutual funds is the way you make money. Down at the bank, savings and loan, or credit union you only have one way which is the interest they pay.

BANKS
SAVINGS AND LOAN   =   INTEREST
CREDIT UNION

With a mutual fund you have three different ways of making money on your money.

The first way I have already touched on and it is called **appreciation of the share price** and it happens when you buy shares and the share price goes up as in the $100 per month example I used earlier.

The second way that you make money is on **dividends**. A dividend is when a company in your mutual fund portfolio makes a profit they send profits to the mutual fund and the mutual fund company disperses those profits as you the investor tell them to. You can either take the dividend in cash or have it re-invested. Of course if you are seeking growth then you will want them re-invested.

Dividends are the area of focus that our current President is actively working to further cut taxes for us. I was driving the boat when he addressed the nation and announced his plans for tax cuts. As soon as the address was over the radio station had a call in program for people to voice their opinions about the address.

One of the first callers was a liberal complaining that the President was only cutting taxes for the rich people who could afford to invest money in the economy. To back that claim up he used the example that common people would not receive the tax breaks because they were not able to invest in stocks. I think maybe that caller could use a good dose of Financial Fitness.

If and when those tax cuts go through even we the small investors will be able to take advantage of them making investing a **$MART** thing to do even before the tax cuts of an IRA. In my opinion those tax cuts are an excellent way to stimulate the economy. By offering tax cuts more people, especially the small investors will want to invest in the American economy.

Already your money is making money two to one compared to the bank, but there is yet another way to make money in a mutual fund. **Capitol gains** are the third and final way to make money in a mutual fund.

A capitol gain is simply the buying of stock low and selling it high. In other words if the professional managers that operate your mutual fund purchased stock in Company "A" at $50 per share and it went up to $75 per share and they decided that it was a good time to sell Company "A" stock then they are going to sell it. The end result for you as an investor is a $25 per share capitol gain, which you can take in cash or have re-invested.

```
MUTUAL FUNDS   =   APPRECIATION OF SHARES
                   DIVIDENDS
                   CAPITOL GAINS
```

YOU MAKE MONEY THREE TO ONE COMPARED TO FINANCIAL INSTITUTIONS.

Different mutual fund companies also have different minimum amounts that you can invest every month. In order to find a company that has a minimum that fits your budget, look in the yellow pages under mutual funds and call each company to find out what the minimum is.

Most of the companies will require you to have $500 or $1,000 to start but some companies will allow you to invest with as little as $25 per month on a systematic investment as long as it is drafted from your checking or savings account every month.

I am not an expert on mutual funds nor will I recommend any one company or any particular fund. These are just the basics in order to get you started.

It is up to you to do the research and find out what your investment goals are and how to accomplish them. Everyone's investment goals will be different. There is a word of warning that I would like to throw in here. Never ever borrow money to invest. The money you invest should be extra money.

Make sure before investing in any particular fund that you have spoken to an agent that is licensed through the Securities Exchange Commission and have received and read a prospectus on the fund that you are interested in. Do not be afraid to ask to see an agent's license, I am sure that they will be glad to show it to you.

Also consult your tax advisor on the tax advantages of investing through an IRA but be careful about discussing particular funds with an advisor that does not have a SEC license. Although a SEC agent gets paid a commission for helping you choose a fund, the field is highly regulated by the government and the agent has to show reasons why they recommended a particular fund. His advice should be in your best interest as an investor. However, should you have questions you can contact:

U.S. Securities and Exchange Commission
450 5th Street N.W
Washington, D.C. 20549

Now it really does not matter who you are or what you make, whether you make $15,000 or $115,000 per year, most of the money you make has already got somewhere to go. You have living expenses, taxes, and insurance premiums that you have to pay. At the end of it all you might be lucky and have a little left over to invest. The problem is that most people are not lucky.

Whatever would be going towards investing is already being spent somewhere else. How many times have you heard the old saying, "I've got too much month left over at the end of the money"? Maybe you have said that yourself. Now that you have a little education on how mutual funds work, the next step is finding out how to free up money to invest for your future.

Of course you already know that by doing the **$MART** thing and investing in an IRA or 401k that you will free up some money that would go to Uncle Sam.

The next place that I would like to investigate to see if you can free up some money is with chapter four, THE NINE-LETTER DIRTY WORD. This chapter will deal with a subject that is essential for financial fitness but one that has been misunderstood to the point of becoming a dirty word.

I hope to shed some light on the subject so that you are never again offended by the nine-letter dirty word.

CHAPTER 4
THE NINE LETTER DIRTY WORD

I have already shown you that by making your investment account into an IRA that you can reduce your taxes which will free up some money for you to invest every year with the help of your tax advisor. That is of course the **$MART** thing to do.

The second place that you can look at to free up additional money to invest is in what I call the nine letter dirty word of the English language. I-N-S-U-R-A-N-C-E! Insurance is a necessary evil, but nobody likes to talk about it. If you are not protecting your family with enough insurance then you are taking a big gamble. Insurance is however a dirty word, if you don't believe me just tell someone that you are an insurance salesman and see what kind of response you get.

We have to have insurance to protect our home, our car, our livelihood, and our family. Have you ever heard someone say, "I don't need anymore insurance, I'm insurance poor"? The reason people say that "I'm insurance poor" is because those people are paying high premiums for a product that they hopefully will never use and more than likely have no understanding of how it works in the first place. Insurance is definitely a dirty word to most people.

The reason people do not understand how the insurance game works is because they never read their policies, and even if they did, the policies are written in such a legal manner that the common person such as you and I can not understand exactly what is being said.

There is a simple explanation to the reason everything is so confusing in an insurance policy. The reason being the smoke and mirrors trick. If someone can charge you more money for a policy and confuse you on the benefits, then they can make more money off of you, the consumer.

In other words less benefits that cost more money. I explained earlier about how an agent with a securities license has to look out for your best interest when helping you choose a fund to invest in. Well, the government regulates the insurance industry also, but there is a difference here. The products that they recommend may not be in your best interest.

Just because it is legal does not mean it is right. Once again I am not going to attack any one person or company, I will give you the facts and you decide what is right and what is wrong. The first place I will start is with life insurance.

CASH VALUE LIFE INSURANCE

As far as life insurance goes, the traditional choice for the last 150 years or so in this country has been what is known as Cash Value life insurance. Now you might have heard this called a lot of different names such as Whole-life, Ordinary life, Universal life, Variable life, or Twenty pay life. Like I said there are a lot of different names for this type of insurance, literally thousands of names for it, but basically it is any kind of life insurance that builds up a savings account inside of the policy. I am sure that you know the kind of policy that I am talking about, it is the kind that you can borrow from.

The premiums for Cash Value life insurance never go up, they stay the same for your whole life, thus the name, "Whole-Life Insurance".

After a few years your policy begins to build a savings account inside of it, if you need some money then you can borrow it at 6-8% interest. At the age of 65 your policy will have enough cash value to trade in and help augment your retirement.

Now there are three things that we all want to do for our families. Number one is to protect our family in case we die. Number two we want to build up an emergency fund in case something comes up so we can get our hands on some cash. Number three we want to have some money for retirement.

THREE THINGS WE WANT TO DO FOR OUR FAMILY

1 **Protect them financially if we die**
2 **Build an emergency fund**
3 **Provide retirement income in case we live**

You see Cash Value life insurance takes care of those three needs. That sounds like a pretty good deal doesn't it? More than likely, if you have purchased this type of life insurance, then that is the basic pitch that you heard.

Now let me tell you the facts. If you own this type of life insurance and you have had it for several years then you also have a savings account building inside of it. Let's say after 10 or so years, that you die. Now you have some money built up in your cash value plus you have the face amount that the company agrees to pay in case you die. Your Family gets both the savings and the face amount, right? Wrong!

In most cases the policy only pays the face amount. All the extra money that you paid in to have the savings account within your policy, the insurance company keeps. Usually on the very first page of your policy it will say that upon your death (the insured) the company (the insurer) agrees to pay the face amount. It does not say the face amount plus the cash value.

In other words, you are paying extra money in order to have two things. You are paying to have the death protection and the savings but your family can only collect one if you die.

If you went to the music store and bought a double-platinum album of you favorite artist and you got home only to find one compact disc in the case what would you think? How fast would you complain? In my opinion if you pay for two things, then you should get two things, would you not agree? So if you're paying extra money to build up your cash value in a life insurance program, shouldn't your family get both if you die? The answer is of course, but that is not the way it works with Cash Value life insurance.

YOUR PREMIUM
PAYS FOR TWO THINGS

FACE AMOUNT	CASH VALUE

IF YOU DIE
THE COMPANY ONLY PAYS ONE

FACE AMOUNT

That is the worst thing about this type of life insurance, but the negatives do go on.

Next is that the money you have in your cash value is restricted. In other words if you need some of the money in your cash value for an emergency, then you have to pay the insurance company 6% and sometimes 8% for the privilege to borrow your money. Who's money are you borrowing? Your money, right? Yes, it is your money; you are paying extra to have a policy that builds cash value, yet if you need that money then you have to borrow it! Who invented that?!?

That is not like having your money in a company sponsored 401k in which you can borrow the money and the interest is paid to yourself into your account. It is in fact paying interest to an insurance company in order to use your own money.

If that extra money were at the bank in savings instead of in your policy in savings would you expect to have to borrow it? The answer is obvious; of course you wouldn't have to borrow your own money.

Then to top that all off, if you did borrow from your policy and died the next day or the next week, guess what? Now they no longer pay the face amount, because they deduct whatever amount you borrowed from the face amount.

IF YOU BORROW FROM YOUR POLICY AND DIE
THE COMPANY NO LONGER PAYS THE ENTIRE FACE AMOUNT

FACE AMOUNT MINUS WHAT YOU OWE

For the sake of example, let's say that I own a bank and you wanted to start a savings account at my bank with $100 per month. Then I told you that for the first three to five years that how ever much money that you decided to put in my bank, in your savings account, that I was going to keep it all just for the price of doing business with me, what would you say? In other words your savings account book would show zero for at least three years. I am sure that you would tell me that I was crazy, and that you would take your business elsewhere.

If you own this type of insurance then flip to the cash value page, the page where it lists how your money grows. Check out how long it takes before you start seeing money in the cash value.

It is more than likely somewhere between 3-5 years. Before that it will all be zeros. I really do not know if I made my point clear, but if I did not, then let me say that you are paying extra money, sometimes more than twice as much, for Cash Value life insurance. So why do you have to wait 3-5 years before you see any money?

YOU PAY EXTRA PREMIUM DOLLARS
IN ORDER TO HAVE CASH VALUE

CASH VALUE 3-5 YEARS-$0 AFTER THAT BORROW @ 6-8%

That's not all; they will pay you for the use of your money, just like the bank will, somewhere between zero and 3% depending on your policy. Remember the quarter of a million-dollar mistake? Oh yea, it works with insurance companies also. As a matter of a fact an insurance policy is the worst place to save your money.

Another reason that you will want to refrain from saving your money in an insurance policy is when it comes to retirement. You have paid all that extra money in, in order to have some extra money for retirement.

When you are ready to retire and draw out your money, you have two choices. First, you can borrow your cash value for retirement, which you already know is not a good idea. Or number two, you can surrender your policy and take the cash value to supplement your retirement. You get all your cash value, but you had to surrender your policy to obtain it.

Again you paid for two things but only got one. Go to Wal*Mart and buy a pair of socks only to discover when you get home that you only have one sock. You paid for two things and only got one!

They call it cash surrender value because you have to give up the coverage in order to get the cash even though you paid for both. So no matter whether you live or whether you die you can only receive one benefit from this type of life insurance.

YOUR PREMIUM
PAYS FOR TWO THINGS

FACE AMOUNT	CASH VALUE

IF YOU LIVE TO RETIRE
YOU HAVE TO SURRENDER THE FACE AMOUNT IN ORDER TO GET
THE CASH VALUE

CASH VALUE
TO AUGMENT RETIREMENT

UNIVERSAL LIFE INSURANCE AND "PAID UP" POLICIES

There are some policies that say that they will pay the face amount plus the savings and they will give you a computer generated sheet about how they think your money will grow. Usually this is in a policy known as Universal life. Universal life usually states right on the front of the policy that it has adjustable premiums and flexible benefits. Really what does that tell you about the policy?

It means that you never know what you are going to have or what you are going to be paying for it. You can bet that if you do not pay enough for your policy, it will lapse and you will no longer have any coverage.

These policies are typically sold with the promise that if you pay a certain amount for a certain amount of years that it will eventually be "paid up" and you will no longer owe any more premiums. In other words you will have free insurance. Are we so naïve as to believe that we can actually get something for free?

What they do not tell you is that after your policy is "paid up" that you still owe premiums they just do not bill you for the premiums. Instead they take the money out of your cash value to cover the premium. Once you run out of cash value then your policy will lapse and you will have no coverage and no cash value. Again you paid for two things but only got one. It works that way every time.

Beware also of the computer-generated figures that are used to sell these policies. They are simply a guess of what they think your policy will accumulate. It is still a form of Cash Value life insurance and it is not like having a prospectus from a mutual fund that shows you what that particular fund has actually done in the past. Life insurance is not a mutual fund.

POLICIES THAT PAY DIVIDENDS

There are some companies out there that you have to join a club in order to receive their insurance. They are known as participating companies, and they are the companies that pay so-called dividends on their policies.

Didn't you learn about dividends in the chapter about mutual funds? This must involve a mutual fund, right? Wrong! You see there are some companies out there that promise you dividends. Well the U.S., Treasury got wind of this and they investigated it. I mean after all, if you are making a profit then Uncle Sam wants his share, right?

The U.S. Treasury Decision, number 1743 (1911) states that, "Dividends declared by participating companies are not dividends in a commercial sense of the word, but are simply refunds to the policyholder of a portion of the overcharge collected".

What that means is, now that you own this book, I am going to make you a member of my club. So every month from now on you send me an extra $5 for no good reason (just because I want to over-charge you for this book) and a year or two or three down the road, when I feel like it, I am going to send you $1. I am going to send you $1 just because I feel like it and I am going to call it a dividend. Does that make sense? Well I guess not!

That's the way that dividends in life insurance work. I could go on and on about these types of policies because as I stated before there are literally thousands of variations. To sum it all up, just remember this rule. Do not buy any life insurance that has a savings or so-called investment attached to it. An insurance company is no place to save money.

So now that we have the facts, what are we gonna do about it. I am about to give you the solution to the problem of Cash Value insurance, but your agent may try to convince you that they have that very solution. You be the judge, and be for sure that you know what you are getting into before you do it. The solution to the problems of Cash Value life insurance is a principle known as BUY TERM AND INVEST THE DIFFERENCE.

TERM LIFE INSURANCE

What you are looking for when it comes to life insurance is what is known as Term insurance. Term insurance is pure life insurance and nothing else. You can purchase term insurance at a fraction of the cost because there is no savings account or cash value building inside the policy.

You are paying for one thing which is life insurance and should you die your family gets what you paid for, the face amount. In other words no savings account and no buying two things and only getting one.

BUY TERM AND INVEST THE DIFFERENCE

If you own Cash Value life insurance like most people do then by replacing it with Term you can free up a lot of money every month to invest in your mutual fund or to pay off high interest debts on your road to financial fitness. Not only that but you can take your cash value out and invest it in a lump sum amount into your mutual fund.

The principal that this was built on states that when you are younger and you do not have a lot of cash, you need a lot of protection for your family in case you die. So buy the most amount of coverage for the least amount of money, which would be Term life insurance, not Cash Value life insurance.

Next, take the extra amount that you would have spent to get the Cash Value insurance and invest it in a mutual fund. The more the mutual fund grows and the more cash you have, the less you need life insurance because you now have the cash.

Eventually you will have enough cash that you will no longer need the life insurance. In other words, life insurance is not something that you need for your "whole life". What would you rather have at retirement-$100,000 worth of life insurance or $100,000 cash? I think the answer is pretty obvious.

You will want to purchase your life insurance from one place and put your savings somewhere else. By separating your insurance from your savings you are paying for two things and if you die your family gets both. If you live until retirement then you do not have to borrow your money to get it or surrender your policy if you do not choose to. You will have paid for two things and you will be able to get two things.

Not to mention that your money will be credited to you immediately, you will not have to put money in for 3-5 years before you see any of it.

Also you will be avoiding the quarter of a million-dollar mistake by controlling your own money instead of letting the insurance company control it for you.

You may have an agent that will tell you that his program is just like BUY TERM AND INVEST THE DIFFERENCE. Well, it's not! There is nothing that is just like BUY TERM AND INVEST THE DIFFERENCE. Just in case I did not make myself clear, there is nothing just like BUY TERM AND INVEST THE DIFFERENCE! It either is or it is not. How do you tell the difference? Do not purchase any life insurance in which your savings grows within the policy no matter how good they make it sound.

My suggestion would be to deal exclusively with a company that sells Term insurance only. How will you know that they only sell Term? Call them up and ask them.

While you are on the phone with them ask them if they have a policy that will build up some cash that you can use in the future. If they do, then avoid them like the plague. Do not buy any insurance that has a savings account. Only deal with a company that sells Term insurance and only Term insurance.

When you start calling, you will find that the companies that deal with Term and only Term are few, and far between, but they are out there. I have even noticed lately on TV an advertisement in which a company will do a search and find the best Term rates for you.

I have not dealt with that service because I have had my Term insurance with the same company for years. The company that I have my Term insurance through however was on the list of companies that they search and get quotes from. This service may cost you a fee but the fee may be worth it.

Keep in mind that no one can show you how to invest the difference in a mutual fund unless that person has a SEC license; you read about that earlier. Do not forget to ask to see it. You may be tempted to ask your agent that you have now to show you how to BUY TERM AND INVEST THE DIFFERENCE. If that agent put you in a Cash Value program to begin with, then are you going to trust him with your financial fitness again?

BUT UNCLE ROB IS MY AGENT

The agent that put you into a Cash Value program may be a friend or family member and you might think that you couldn't change your program because of emotional ties. All I have to say to that is, does Uncle Rob pay your bills and will he be there to support you when you retire?

Let's face it, money is money and if you do not look out for your best interest, who will? I want you to know how devastating to your financial future and how serious that this type of life insurance is to you no matter who sold it to you.

That brings me to one of the final things that your insurance agent may use to make sure that you buy Cash Value life insurance instead of Term. The agent may agree with you that BUY TERM AND INVEST THE DIFFERENCE sounds good on paper, but really can people actually invest the difference without being forced to?

In plain English do you have the discipline to make sure that you put the extra money away to insure your families financial fitness? The agent might tell you that since you are already used to putting money away in the cash value program that was sold to you and since you have changed programs that you might spend the money instead of investing it.

So what if you do? At least you have gotten a little pleasure out of it instead of giving it to someone who keeps it if you die. Put the money in a Mason jar, it will do you a lot more good than letting the insurance company have it. If you have an agent that says that you have to be forced to save your money in his program then essentially he is saying that you do not have enough intelligence about you to save for your own family's future.

If you really do need to be forced to invest the difference, then have the extra money taken out of your paycheck by payroll deduction and put into your 401K plan or have your investments automatically drawn from your checking account by draft and put into a systematic investment program. Whatever you do, separate the two and do not save your money inside a policy.

Most people save money with financial institutions instead of investing in the economy and most people own cash value life insurance as well. Most people also retire broke. Do you think that there is any relationship between where they put their money all their life and how they end up at retirement? Do you think rich people do the same things with their money that you are doing with yours? Those are definitely questions worth pondering.

If I have not convinced you that BUY TERM AND INVEST THE DIFFERENCE is not a better way to go then go to the library and read up on the subject. There are countless books and newspaper articles that say the same thing that I have told you here.

As a matter of a fact the only ones that recommend Cash Value Life Insurance are usually the people that sell it.
There are however, a few rules that go with BUY TERM AND INVEST THE DIFFERENCE and here they are:

BUY TERM AND INVEST THE DIFFERENCE RULES

1-Make sure that you do invest the difference, so that you are not another statistic as to why not to follow this plan.

2-Do not purchase Annual Re-newable Term insurance. If you do then you may have to prove insurability on a yearly basis, and your premium will go up every year. Look for Level Term for at least 10- 20 years, in which the premiums and face amount stay the same for that long. This is available call the companies and ask for it.

3-Do not buy Decreasing Term in which your benefits go down every year unless you are up in age and this is all that you can afford.

4-Never and I mean NEVER, cancel a life insurance policy until another company has approved you. Cash Value Insurance is better than no insurance at all. Make sure that you prove insurability. If you have Cash Value life of any type, then you need to replace it. But do not cancel it until you have the new policy. You will have a 10-20 day free look without cost or obligation.

5-READ YOUR POLICY!

6-Determine how much Term insurance you need- The basic rule of thumb is to multiply your annual gross income by 8. That will give you a rough idea of how much you need to replace your income for your family if you die. That amount should be sufficient if invested to provide your family with enough money every month to replace your income. However, you also have to take into consideration how much personal debt you have. If you have a lot of personal debt you may want to consider additional life insurance.

_____ X 8 = BASIC FACE AMOUNT NEEDED
(ANNUAL INCOME)

With that being said, you and I have explored two ways to free up money to invest. First was by reducing your tax burden with an IRA, and the second way was by saving money on life insurance.

Before we get off of the nine-letter dirty word of the English language I have just one final suggestion on how to free up money to invest as far as insurance goes.

RAISE YOUR DEDUCTIBLES

On your health, car and homeowner's, you can save a lot of money with two easy steps each. Shop around for the best rates and raise your deductibles. It is that simple.

Do not be fooled by an agent telling you that if you have all your insurance with them that the price will be cheaper. An agent can not legally discount insurance, or pay part of your premium, or give you any gifts for doing business with them. It is illegal. The more insurance you buy then the cheaper the rate per thousand (or units) may be. For an agent to tell you that if you have your homeowner's, life, health, and car with them that you will get a cheaper rate overall then just call the insurance commissioner, because it is simply not true. That leaves you free to shop around and find the lowest rate for each type of insurance even if you have to do so through several different companies.

Another effective and creative way to bring down the cost of these insurance products is by raising the deductible. However, do not raise your deductibles unless you have enough cash in a money market account or in cash money to cover that deductible in case something does happen.

That pretty much covers the nine-letter dirty word and what you can be done in order to avoid the bad situations that can be devastating to your financial fitness. There are still some other ways to free up money to invest.

That will bring you to another chapter that I am going to name A LITTLE LAGNIAPPE. Lagniappe is a Creole word that is used in Louisiana a lot and it simply means a little something extra. In the next chapter you will discover the little extra ways to free up money that you did not know you had in order to invest for your financial fitness.

GIVE HIM A BRAKE

In 1872, George Westinghouse asked Cornelius Vanderbilt, multimillionaire President of the New York Central Railroad, to listen to his ideas about developing an "air brake".
Vanderbilt wrote back:

"I have no time to waste on fools.-Vanderbilt"

After the brake was successfully tested on another railroad, Vanderbilt wrote Westinghouse asking to see it.
Westinghouse wrote back:

"I have no time to waste on fools.-Westinghouse"

- Excerpt from a Bathroom Reader

CHAPTER 5
A LITTLE LAGNIAPPE

Just as a quick review you already know that by investing in an IRA you can take advantage of tax shelters thus reducing your tax burden every year. You can **$**ave **M**oney **A**nd **R**educe **T**axes. Also by buying the right kind of life insurance and raising the deductibles on your other insurance programs that you can free up money to invest.

So far if you are like most people then you already have the knowledge to free up a lot of money to invest in a good nest egg for your financial fitness. Just with those principles alone you could, and probably will retire in a lot better shape, if you take advantage of the information and apply the principles that you have learned.

Still there are other ways to increase your financial fitness and free up money to invest. A little lagniappe if you will. This chapter is dedicated to the other little things that you can do to ensure financial success. These are by far the most exciting and fun principles covered in this book.

There will come a time when you start seeing your investments grow and you will have assets where you once had liabilities. I pray that the time comes soon for you and I know that it will. Your next goal of course is to increase your worth and reduce your liabilities. Let's explore some fundamental ways to do just that.

Most Americans on average have over $15,000 of unsecured debt besides their mortgage. This is the debt (death) trap. Everywhere you go you see and hear advertisements to buy on credit with payments being a small amount per month. You can get what you want now and pay for it later in installments. It seems that the payments do not amount to that much every month, but when you figure it up with credit cards, department store cards, gas cards, finance companies and other loan payments, most people have more than they can reasonably handle every month.

Personally I believe that all debt is bad. Any time that you are working a certain percentage of your week just to pay someone else then it limits your life style. It is so much easier to pay cash for what you obtain and be done with it.

Debt to most people has become a necessity instead of a convenience. A lot of people have to use debt in order to pay other debts just to stay caught up. Hence the phrase "Rob Peter to pay Paul". Debt is something that has become socially acceptable when in fact it should make you angry. Every time you see an ad or watch a commercial asking you to get further in debt it should offend you. They are in fact asking you to work for them a certain amount of your week.

Not only that, even though they give you small payments, they usually charge you a high rate of interest. In most cases you are paying 18-21% on your unsecured debts. Remember the number 72?

Money problems have been the major cause of a lot of divorces as well as suicides. Debt can and will reduce the quality of your life and leave you broke and unhappy.

I realize that for most people paying in cash for everything is out of the question but I believe that you should continue to strive to be completely debt free. I further believe that being debt free is probably most people's number one financial goal. Why else would you invest your time and money in books like this one.

When you put money in the bank at 3-5% (which with today's economy you can't even get that) and borrow money at 18-21% then money is working harder against you than it is for you.

No wonder people have their back against the wall and the only light they see at the end of the tunnel is a train. The problem with all the unsecured debt is the interest that they charge and the minimum payments that you pay every month.

Basically if you pay the minimums every month most of the money that you pay goes to interest and very little towards paying off the principle, which leaves you spending a lifetime paying the minimums and you will never get out of debt. Watch your credit card statements if you pay the minimum payment and you will discover that every month little or no money goes toward reducing the principle.

So what can be done about this problem? There are several things that you can do. The first is, do not use debt anymore and operate on a cash only basis. The only way that you can get out of debt is by not incurring debt any more and by paying off what you already owe. Yes, I know that is a mouth full and it seems much easier to say than do. Don't worry I'm not just going to say it I will teach you how to operate on a cash only basis later in the book. For now let's look at simple things that
Can be done to reduce your debt.

ASK FOR A LOWER INTEREST RATE

On the back of your credit cards you will find a toll free number that you can call for customer service. Simply call them up and ask for a lower interest rate. In most cases if you have had the account for awhile and made timely payments they will drop the interest rate a few percentage points. Actually this is like putting a band-aide on a crack in a dam, but hey every little bit helps, and at least your are taking steps to reduce your liabilities and improve your financial fitness.

There are two other things that you can do that will drastically reduce your personal debt. Both of the ideas will be discussed in more detail later in this book but for now I want to cover them quickly and give you time to roll them over in your mind until you get to the chapter where you actually apply them.

THE DEBT ELIMINATOR

The first thing you can do to drastically reduce your personal debt is what I will call the DEBT ELIMINATOR. This principle requires that you either use some of the money that you have freed up or find a way to make some extra money in order to reduce debt.

Personally I recommend that you find a legal way to make an extra $100 per month or more for this purpose. In a later chapter we will concentrate on finding $100 extra per month and this will be one of the first things you will use it for.

All you have to do after you have earmarked $100 per month for getting out of debt is to start with the debt that you owe the least on. Apply that extra $100 per month plus the regular payment every month to that debt until it is paid off.

After you have the first account paid off you can move on to the second one. Begin paying the $100 per month plus the regular payment previously spent on the first debt plus the regular payment of the second one and apply all that money to the second account until it is paid off.

Do you see how you can pay off some debts very quickly with just a little extra effort? You can keep doing this process until you have paid off all your personal debt, and then apply all that money to your mortgage.

This process is like stepping on the accelerator and driving towards financial fitness. It is simple but it is not easy, it takes commitment.

This will not only accelerate getting out of debt it will also build self-esteem and confidence. Every time that you pay off one account you will feel a sense of pride and will be excited to get started on the next account.

Make sure each time that you pay an account off that you celebrate. Take your spouse out to a nice place to eat and enjoy the thought of being one more step closer to financial fitness. Be sure that you pay cash for dinner and do not put it on a credit card.

REGULAR PAYMENTS ON ACCOUNT #1 PLUS $100 PER MONTH UNTIL ACCOUNT #1 IS PAID IN FULL

REGULAR PAYMENTS ON ACCOUNT #2 PLUS THE REGULAR PAYMENTS PREVIOUSLY SPENT ON ACCOUNT #1 PLUS 100 PER MONTH UNTIL ACCOUNT #2 IS PAID IN FULL

CONTINUE THE ELIMINATION PROCESS UNTIL YOU HAVE NO PERSONAL DEBT.

There is a down side to the DEBT ELIMINATOR if it is not done properly. If you are still used to using debt for everything and you begin to pay off an account then you may feel like you can charge even more on that account. If you do this then you are actually going to a lot of trouble with no benefits.

My suggestion is that while you are in this process that you remove all charge account cards from your wallet and put them in a box out of sight. Do not keep any cards with you and do not charge anything.

Once you pay an account off have a card cutting ceremony as part of your celebration and know that you will never be claimed by the debt of that account ever again.

If you do choose the DEBT ELIMINATOR as a means for reducing personal debt then you will be less likely to charge on your accounts again. You are working toward a big goal with a lot of little goals in between that will make you appreciate it more than if you had a quick fix.

RE-POSITION YOUR ASSETS

The second way that you can drastically reduce your personal debt is to RE-POSITION YOUR ASSETS. This is actually a quick fix but if done properly can and will take care of the problem as well.

What I mean by RE-POSITION YOUR ASSETS is, if you own a home and have equity in your home then you can actually use that equity to pay off those high interest accounts.

There are four distinct advantages to taking this approach. The first advantage is that you lower the interest rate on the unsecured debt by securing it with your home. This will save you literally thousands of dollars in interest in the long run.

Second is the convenience of having one payment every month that should be lower than the amount that you are currently paying for your mortgage plus all the minimums. That in itself will free up money on a monthly basis to invest for your future in a systematic investment.

The third advantage is that you will know exactly when you will be out of debt. Unlike paying the minimum amounts on your credit cards, the debt will be tied to your mortgage and when the mortgage is paid off, you will be debt-free.

The final advantage may be that you can deduct the interest at tax time because the debt is now covered under your mortgage. That will qualify this idea as being **$MART** because once again you can **$**ave **M**oney **A**nd **R**educe **T**axes thus freeing up money that you would normally pay Uncle Sam.

The laws concerning this tax advantage are always changing so consult your tax advisor to find out if the interest will be tax deductible. If so then that is more money that you can invest towards financial fitness.

Of course, there are some down sides to the quick fix method that I have just described as RE-POSITION YOUR ASSETS. This quick fix will hurt you more than it will help you if you continue to incur debt. You have to make a commitment to not charge on your accounts ever again if you decide to re-position your assets and tie your unsecured debt into your mortgage. You will have to cut up all of your credit cards.

The problem with most people is that they refinance and lower their monthly payments and it was so quick and so easy that they forgot how devastating it was to be in the financial bind that they were in to begin with. So not only do they start spending the extra money every month that they have freed up, they also begin charging on the accounts again that they have just paid off.

Before they know it all their accounts are maxed out again and now their mortgage cost them more every month on top of it all.

Do not rush out and refinance your home and use this idea unless you are ready to cut up all of your credit cards and never use debt again. You can not get out of debt by continuing to incur debt, no matter how you re-position your assets.

Also let me say again that you should not try any of these ideas until you have read the entire set of instructions for your paycheck. As I have mentioned before you will learn how to operate on a cash only basis later in this book. If you do a step out of line then it could have a negative effect instead of a positive one. Be patient and soon you will begin to see how to apply what you have learned. For now just keep this idea in the back of your mind then you will decide later after you have created a plan on paper if re-positioning your assets is something that you should consider.

KNOW YOUR MORTGAGE

There are a few other things that get hidden in the paperwork when you are dealing with your mortgage that you need to be aware of before you decide to consolidate your debt and tie it into your mortgage. A lot of these I have to admit I learned the hard way through trial and error.

There are closing costs anytime that you re-finance your home. With most lenders the closing cost and legal fees are included inside the mortgage so there are no out-of-pocket expenses. It makes it easy for you to re-finance but keep in mind that if you continue to incur debt on your accounts and re-finance it with your home every time your accounts are maxed out then these costs raise your mortgage every time also. You will in fact be caught in a debt (death) trap.

Also most lenders have a pre-payment penalty, which means if you pay the loan off early then you have to pay extra money, sometimes thousands of dollars. So if you re-position your assets and pay off your mortgage in the process then you may get hit with this extra charge.

You will have to weigh out the difference between how much interest you will have to pay over the life of your unsecured debt as opposed to what you will have to pay in pre-payment penalties.

If your pre-payment penalties are excessively high then I would recommend that you stick with the debt accelerator.

If you are offered an exceptionally low interest rate then there are two things that you need to look for in the paperwork.

THE LOWEST POSSIBLE FIXED RATE

First is a balloon note and the second is an adjustable rate. The balloon note means that after a certain number of years that your mortgage will be due in full. Imagine the surprise when you do not realize that you have a balloon note and all of a sudden one day you discover that you owe the balance of your mortgage in full. This can happen if you do not read the contract at closing then years later you realize that the balloon just went pop in your face.

What you are left with is to either pay your mortgage off in full or re-finance it possibly at a higher interest rate, but definitely with all the closing costs associated with it.

The adjustable rate simply means what it says; the interest rate can go up and down according to the prime interest rate. This route is wonderful when the rate goes down, but when it goes up it is very disappointing. You will never know from one year to the next exactly what you will be paying in interest. Personally I believe that even if the interest rate starts out a little higher, by obtaining a fixed rate mortgage that you will be more aware of exactly what is going on with your finances.

A fixed rate mortgage means the interest rate will stay the same for the life of the mortgage. That is the point of this entire book which is to find out exactly where you are, exactly where you want to go, and make a plan for getting there with as few surprises as possible.

Of course there are some of you who are educated on creative finance techniques and for some situations a balloon note or an adjustable rate may be the right tool to use. In general and for the rest of us the lowest possible fixed rate will be the best route to go with a mortgage.

RETAIN A LAWYER

Nevertheless do not sign any contracts until you have retained a lawyer and your lawyer, not theirs, has read the contract and explained it to you fully. This will be an extra cost on your part but you are talking about a huge chunk of your financial future when it comes to your mortgage. It is always worth the money to get legal advice.

Since you already have a need for a lawyer the time is right to go ahead and have a will drawn up. By owning a will you are ensuring that your wishes are followed in the event of your death. That way what you have worked hard for is not included in your estate with some one else having control over it.

A 30-YEAR MORTGAGE?

When you are dealing with mortgages you will also have to decide on the life of the mortgage. In my studies it has been recommended by countless experts to obtain a mortgage with the least amount of years to pay and to avoid a thirty-year mortgage at all costs.

The reason that you want fewer years is that you have less time to pay on the loan so there is less interest to be paid. That makes sense, but the problem is that most people can not afford the payments on a fifteen or seven-year mortgage. If you have got or have to obtain a thirty-year mortgage and can afford the payments comfortably then that is great. There is still something that you can do to cut down the number of years that you have to pay on that mortgage thus cutting down the total amount of interest that you will pay.

THE MORTGAGE ACCELERATOR

I am about to describe how to speed up, or accelerate your mortgage. This is a very simple procedure that will require a little time but the effect will be well worth what you put into it.

The way it works is by paying a half payment on your mortgage every two weeks instead of a full payment every month. It seems to be the same amount of money when in fact, because of the five-week months in the year; you actually end up paying an extra payment every year.

What that will do is take literally years off the life of a thirty-year mortgage and save you thousands in interest.

Now if you go down to the bank or finance company and start trying to pay them a half payment you will be met with some resistance. In most cases you are not allowed to do this.

You may end up having to set up your checking or savings account in a way that you earmark a half payment every two weeks for this purpose. Pay it once per month and explain when you pay the extra that it should go to the principle on your mortgage. It never fails that the teller will explain that even though you are paying extra on your account that the full payment will be due next month. They may try to discourage you from making these extra payments because that means they are losing interest in the long run. Do not be discouraged, be courteous and continue to work your plan.

If doing it that way is too much trouble for you then you can just accumulate enough money for an extra payment every year to accomplish this goal and that is fine. The reason that it is explained as a half payment every two weeks is because you can see it as being the same amount of money as a whole payment every month. The extra payment comes over the period of a year and it does not put you into a financial bind to do it.

While we are dealing with the subjects of mortgages and unsecured debt I must digress for a moment and cover something about the nine-letter dirty word.

THE NINE-LETTER DIRTY WORD RE-VISITED

Insurance is something that will come up when you obtain credit and you can get the raw end of the deal here also. The companies that you obtain credit or mortgages from will most always try to tack on a little lagniappe for themselves in the form of credit life insurance. For example if you purchase a home for $100,000 the company will want you to have and a lot of times will require you to have life insurance to cover that amount if you die.

They can require you to have it but they can not legally require you to have the life insurance that they offer. Credit life works pretty much like decreasing term insurance.

In other words you will purchase $100,000 worth of life insurance that will be included in your mortgage payment. After you pay on your mortgage let's say for ten years and for the sake of example you now only owe $75,000 on your mortgage. You are still paying premiums for $100,000 but the insurance will only pay the balance, which is $75,000.

The solution to this problem is to not obtain credit life insurance. If you are planning to purchase a home increase your personal life insurance to cover it. That way if you have $100,000 worth of 15 or 20 year term and you die in ten years the policy still pays $100,000 instead of $75,000.

This does not just apply to mortgages you more than likely have credit life on your unsecured debt as well. Credit card companies are bad about calling with a pitch to sell some sort of insurance to their "valued" customers. You, Mr. Consumer, can have this insurance for free for the first three months and after that it is only a few dollars per month. Does that sound familiar? The problem with that is that most of the time the type of insurance that they are selling you will never pay off.

The insurance deals that come with credit card companies are usually accidental death policies. That means that if you die from natural causes the policy will not pay. It is a little on the morbid side to check the obituaries in your local paper, but if you do then you will see how many people actually die of accidents. From my research I have found that most people die of natural causes.

Companies will also sometimes offer double indemnity policies. Double indemnity means that they will pay a certain amount if you die of natural causes and will double it if you die of an accident. With your personal insurance program it will pay the same no matter how you die unless that is the type of personal insurance you have. The point to all this is if you need $100,000 worth of life insurance, get a $100,000 and do not gamble on your family's future on how you will die.

Also when you purchase insurance from one of these companies that means that less of your payment is going toward paying off your debt. If you have credit life insurance it is obvious that you need to replace it by increasing your personal program. By increasing your life insurance you will likely decrease the rate per thousand that you have to pay and that in turn may be cheaper for you than what you are paying on credit life right now. If that is the case then you will free up more money to invest or put toward the reduction of debt.

UNCLE SAM IS NOT SANTA CLAUSE

There are a lot of ways, literally hundreds of ways to free up money. Another way that is lagniappe is by not giving the government an interest free loan. Every year people pay extra money in to Uncle Sam just so they can get a refund at the end of the year. People actually feel like they are getting something for nothing when actually it is their money all the time.

Uncle Sam is not Santa Clause and taxes are not Christmas club accounts. If you owe income taxes and you do not pay then you get charged interest, yet the government uses the extra money that you send them and they do not pay any interest. That is worst than saving your money in a bank.

Does it not make more sense to pay as little as possible during the year and put the remainder into an interest bearing account? By doing this you will actually make money. Make sure however, that if you do lessen the amount taken out during the year that you do set aside money in an account to ensure that you have enough to pay what you owe at the end of the year. You may even want to do your taxes every quarter so you do not have to pay it all in one lump sum at the end of the year.

CLEAR THE SMOKE

Other ways that you can free up money to invest are more personal in nature. Say for example, if you are a smoker, by becoming smoke-free, you can free up a lot of money that will grow and you can improve your financial fitness as well as your health.

As a popular radio talk show host would put it I am now typing this out with my formerly nicotine-stained fingers. I recently became a non-smoker and although it was by far one of the most difficult things I ever set out to do, the rewards are definitely worth the sacrifice. One main reason for setting and accomplishing this goal is the financial aspect.

At present cigarettes on average cost about $3.00 per pack and I smoked approximately 1 pack per day. $3.00 x 7 days per week = $21 per week x 52 weeks per year = $1092 per year that I spent on cigarettes. Now I am investing that money instead. If I get an average of a 12% return then I will have a lot of lagniappe. Let me show you what accomplishing this goal means to me.

$1092 per year at 12%
Number of years: 10 years   20 years   30 years   40 years
Would grow to: $21,462 $88,122 $295,158 $938,183

Not only am I able to reap the benefits of investing the money that I was previously spending on cigarettes but after a year of being tobacco free my life insurance rates will be reduced by almost half. That is even more lagniappe that can be invested or used to raise the amount of coverage that I have.

Just by changing one habit you can paint a whole different financial picture. This was money that I was just burning up. I had a personal goal to become smoke-free that was also a financial goal.

I do not wish to spend time telling you to quit smoking because it is a personal decision, but that is a powerful reason to at least consider it.

Before you are finished you will be asked to analyze where you are at financially and exactly what you are spending money on. At that point you may find a lot of lagniappe for yourself. For example if you are spending more money on eating out than you are on groceries then you may analyze that and make a decision not to eat out as much.

Nevertheless it is extremely important to find out where you are and exactly what you are doing financially so that you can find and recognize the lagniappe that you never knew you had. Finding the extras will be exciting, personal and up to you to change. But I am getting ahead of myself. Shortly you will learn how to analyze your entire financial picture but for now we still have a couple of financial fitness techniques to discover.

In chapter 6, ACCELERATE YOUR INCOME, you will be asked to do one of the hardest things in this book, find a way to accelerate your income. It is a challenge, but I am sure that if you are serious about financial fitness that you will meet this challenge like the champion I am sure that you are.

CHAPTER 6
ACCELERATE YOUR INCOME

$100 EXTRA PER MONTH

In chapter 5 you were introduced to THE DEBT ELIMINATOR in which you were shown how an extra $100 per month could greatly accelerate the rate at which you become debt free. Now it is time to find that $100 per month because it will be critical in the remaining steps of this book.

For some of you the idea of finding an extra $100 per month may seem impossible. Some might say if I only had an extra $100 per month then I wouldn't need FINANCIAL FITNESS. For others finding the extra money will be simple and for others it may already be freed up from some of the techniques that have been covered throughout this book.

I at one time stocked shelves at a grocery store for an extra $100 per month. I really hated that job because I was doing a dead-end job for minimum wage in the public eye. A grown man doing the same job that high-school kids were doing and I couldn't hide from my friends and neighbors when they came in to shop.

The worst part about the job however was at Christmas time when the same Christmas songs were played over and over again through the PA system. I never quite got over that experience and to this day I still do not like Christmas songs.

I did however endure and I stocked groceries for as long as I had to. That is why I know that if you are willing to sacrifice and maybe even do something that you hate that you can make the extra money that you need to work your plans. Do not let pride hold you back because pride definitely will not pay your bills.

I have a friend that used to get up at 4:00 in the morning to deliver newspapers for an extra $100 per month. That particular friend was making over $750,000 per year the last time I saw him and was on track to make over 1,000,000 the next year. Now that is a very unique example, my friend was fortunate enough to get in on the ground floor of a business that is now a Fortune 500 company. The moral of the story is that in the 1970's when he needed to, he found a way to earn an extra $100 per month and you can too.

Making an extra $100 per month may be a challenge for you but I never said working toward financial fitness was easy. I recommend that you find a moral, legal way that you can obtain this extra money. If you do something illegal or immoral to obtain extra money then you will be sabotaging yourself. Eventually it will catch up with you and you will pay a far greater price than what you earned.

At this time let your creative juices flow and explore your talents. I am confident that if you are serious about obtaining financial fitness that you will be able to accomplish this goal.

EXPLORE YOUR TALENTS

Fix something, build something, create something. If you have specialized knowledge in a certain field then write a book like I am doing. If you play an instrument, you can give lessons in your spare time or find someone that you can do demo work for. The possibilities are vast. Maybe you are a people person and can get into part-time sales or you know about real estate and can make money as an investor. If you are mechanically inclined then you can do shade tree mechanic work.

You like everyone else in this world have talents. Put your talents to work and make them profitable. The only person holding you back is yourself.

If you feel like you do not posses a profitable talent then you can always stock shelves at a grocery store for extra money. That statement should be enough inspiration for you to examine, identify, and use something that you are talented at for extra money. The possibilities are endless and once you begin you may even surprise yourself.

GET RICH QUICK

This is not a get-rich-quick-scheme it will take you some time to accomplish your goals. The more money per month that you are able to allocate to these plans then the quicker the results will be.

With that in mind avoid any get-rich-quick-schemes that you run across while searching for a way to come up with extra money. I have investigated a lot of these schemes in my search for financial fitness and for the most part those programs end up costing money with very little or no return. If it sounds too good to be true then it more than likely is. I still have a few of the programs on my bookshelf now and I would not even give them away much less sell them because I would not want anyone else to go through the financial loss and disappointments that I experienced.

Be careful also of stuffing envelopes and assembling products at home. There may be some legitimate opportunities in that area but for the most part all I have seen were scams.

In the same respect do not depend on the lottery or winning at the casino or even an inheritance to catapult you to financial fitness. When you play the lottery or go to the casino the odds are not in your favor and the chance of coming out ahead is not worth risking your financial fitness on.

In 1993 I was living in the state of Georgia when the state lottery was voted on and passed. I purchased a bingo game with the rotating ball that held numbered plastic pills and used it to choose my numbers for the drawing every week.

Every week I played $5 and every week I won my money back. For weeks I won back the $5 I had played.

After doing that for a while I reasoned that if I increased the amount of money I spent buying tickets that I would also increase my return. So I got the bright idea of buying $100 worth of the lottery tickets.

It took me the entire week with my little toy bingo game to draw and fill out the forms for $100 worth of tickets. It was very time consuming but I did in fact buy the tickets before the next drawing.

It was with great excitement that I sat down in front of the TV on the night of the drawing to get the numbers off the lottery show. Little did I realize that only half the work was over. Once I had the winning numbers in hand my next step was the laborious task of going through $100 worth of tickets and comparing the numbers. Because I had to check for any winning combinations that job took me a couple of days but I went at it with enthusiasm; sure that I was going to win big.

Imagine my disbelief and disappointment when I finally finished checking all those tickets only to discover that I hadn't won big. As a matter of fact I didn't even win $1.

At that point and time in my life $100 was a major investment that was hard to come by and I had lost every dime of my so-called investment. I was, to say the least, heart broken.

A good friend of mine tried to help my feelings by reminding me of the fact that a good portion of the money from the lottery went to schools and would benefit children throughout the state. I must admit at that point and time benevolence had not yet seized me and his words did not comfort me very much. After all I was a person that needed to win $100 not lose $100.

The silver lining to the dark cloud of my lottery story is that I learned early not to gamble away money that I needed or wanted for other purposes and now I very seldom buy lottery tickets.

If you spend money at casinos or on the lottery and it does not interfere with your life then by all means have fun at it.

However if you gamble away money that you need and it causes problems in your life then you are destroying your chance at financial fitness and you should seek immediate help. If the latter is the case then please seek help by calling the following number:

1-877-770-7867

As far as an inheritance goes, you can always be written out of a will or your 90-year-old, rich uncle may live to be 120.

Be patient and work with what you have. If it really is impossible for you to obtain an extra $100 per month then accumulate what you can. If it is only $30 per month then you will just have to work the plan longer.

Most anyone can come up with $30 per month extra. That is only roughly $1 per day. Once you have a working plan for obtaining extra money every month then you can apply that money to the instructions that you will find through out the remainder of this book.

There will be an idea in the next chapter that will require the use of $100 per month in order to improve your credit and your relationship with the bank. So let's move on to chapter 7, BANKING ON FINANCIAL FITNESS.

T.J.Kent Music

JUST DROP ME OFF IN NASHVILLE
WRITTEN BY T.J.KENT

WELL MUSIC CITY HERE I COME
I'M RIDING IN TONIGHT
AND YOU MIGHT GET THE BEST OF ME
BUT YOU'RE IN FOR A FIGHT
'CAUSE I JUST GET THIS FEELING
SOMEDAY I'M GONNA WIN
I'M GONNA BE ON THE CMA
WITH A SONG IN THE TOP 10

CHORUS:

JUST DROP ME OFF IN NASHVILLE
WITH A GUITAR IN MY HAND
I'VE BEEN WRITING ALL THESE SONGS
AND I'VE GOT ME A PLAN
ONE OF THESE DAYS I'M GONNA MAKE A MILLION
I'M GONNA MAKE IT, SON
JUST DROP ME OFF IN NASHVILLE
AND WATCH ME GET IT DONE

HEY MISTER CAN'T YOU SEE
THE STARS IN MY EYES
I AIN'T GOT NO MONEY
IT'S EITHER DO IT NOW OR DIE
MAMA CRIED WHEN I LEFT HOME
AND THAT CAUSED A LOT OF PAIN
BUT ONE OF THESE DAYS WHEN I'M WELL-KNOWN
MAMA, THOSE TEARS WON'T BE IN VAIN

CHORUS(repeat twice)

YEA, JUST LET ME OUT RIGHT HERE BOYS

©T.J.Kent Music, 1995
MEMBER NSAI/BMI

IT'S NOT A SIN TO BE RICH-IT'S A MIRACLE

CHAPTER 7
BANKING ON FINANCIAL FITNESS

The goal of FINANCIAL FITNESS is to teach you how to avoid the debt (death) trap and operate on a cash only basis. Also you have learned better places to put your money than in a savings account. So if you are not going to incur anymore debt or save money with the bank then why should you worry about improving your credit or your relationship with the bank?

The answers will become obvious as we progress. The bank in time may be able to help you accelerate your plans toward financial fitness thus a good relationship with the bank and good credit is critical.

Of course I do not know your particular situation, you may have good credit, bad credit, no credit, or you may have filed bankruptcy. Personally, I have experienced all four. Good credit is by far the best of the four. Nevertheless you can always improve your credit and in this chapter you will learn some creative ways to do that.

You can never have too much credit unless you have a lot of credit that is maxed out and you can't afford the monthly payments. From now on, however you will use your credit as an asset instead of a liability. You will no longer incur debt but you will re-position some of your assets through the use of your credit.

BANKRUPTCY?

Are you plagued by debt? Do you get harassing phone calls from creditors? Then just call the law offices of Duey, Cheetam, and Howe and stop the harassment with a chapter 13 bankruptcy.

Sounds simple doesn't it? You can have a clean slate and start all over again. Bam, all your debts are wiped away in one easy stroke.

NEVER, EVER FILE FOR BANKRUPTCY. For some people bankruptcy seems like the only way out of financial difficulties. The old "Hail Mary" when the clock is ticking off the final seconds of the game and you are still down by six points. Your financial fitness is not a game and bankruptcy is not an option.

Some of you even as you are reading this, are considering bankruptcy. **DON'T DO IT!** That's easy for me to say I'm not in your situation. No, I'm not in your situation but I have been through bankruptcy. In hindsight there were other options that I could not see at the time.

You have to find another route besides bankruptcy. Bankruptcy only makes things worse; it is a quick fix that does nothing to correct the actions that got you there to begin with. It teaches you nothing about how to stop incurring debt so the problem is still there.

Remember, the only way to get out of debt is to pay off what you owe and do not use debt anymore. If you use a quick fix then before long you will find yourself right back in debt and filing for bankruptcy again. Finance companies will make sure that you get back in to debt toot-sweet. Have you seen on TV or read in the paper where they offer credit no matter what your credit history? Bankruptcy is not a problem if you are looking to get into more debt.

Bankruptcy will not solve your problems but will only serve to intensify them. After filing for bankruptcy you will have a sense of failure, defeat and embarrassment that will be more harassing than all those creditors that keep calling you. On top of everything it will be on your credit history for ten years.

A lot can happen in ten years and there may be great opportunities out there that are simply not available to you if you file bankruptcy. Do not follow the path of least resistance because things are likely to get tough again and the only escape that you will find is the same old quick fix.

Take charge now, let your creditors know that you have a plan for financial fitness and that you will pay them as soon as possible. If you are really sincere about financial fitness then you will at the end of this book have workable plans of action that will keep you out of bankruptcy.

Once again this will not be easy and you may even find yourself in court being sued for past-due bills. Have your plans with you when you go in front of the judge and explain that you have a workable plan for paying your creditors and becoming debt free. Then do whatever you have to do in order to pay those bills and avoid bankruptcy.

CREDIT COUNSELORS?

Recently there has been a rash of commercials advertising credit-counseling services. These services will work with your creditors in order to lower your monthly payments. Some creditors will cut interest rates and sometimes will even reduce principle in order to get paid through these services.

The result is a lower monthly payment that you can presumably afford paid to the counseling service. The service in turn disperses that money every month to each of your creditors until the full amounts that were agreed upon by your creditors are satisfied. I am sure that there is a fee for this service but I am not certain how it is paid.

These services give you a type of debt consolidation. During the period that you are dealing with the counseling service you have to agree not to incur anymore debt thus eventually you should be debt free. This is advertised as an alternative to bankruptcy and using such a service is far better than filing for bankruptcy.

However I still do not recommend this unless bankruptcy is the only other option. Using a credit counseling service will still effect your credit. These services have advertisements that say that your credit will not be ruined. That's not the same, as saying that it will not be effected.

Your credit will reflect that you had to use a counseling service to gain control of your finances. That will be on your credit report for seven years instead of the ten that comes with bankruptcy. Either way you go you are limited in future endeavors.

If at all possible avoid using this type of service. Instead use what you have already learned and what you will learn in the remainder of this book and apply it in order to become debt free on your own.

If you have already filed for bankruptcy or are using a credit counseling service then go ahead and do what you have to do in order to fulfill your obligations and then re-build your credit as soon as possible. Hold your head up high and know that you are in the process of becoming debt free.

Keep in mind that debt, bankruptcy or the use of a counseling service in no way defines your character. No one will kill you or put you in prison just because you had to file for bankruptcy, so for the most part you are okay.

I just noticed on TV a popular star that is considering filing for bankruptcy. How do you go bankrupt on $50,000,000 per year? It's easy, all you have to do is spend $51,000,000 per year. Now I might consider trying to send him a copy of this book but I think he has a lot of other issues to deal with before he gets to personal finances.

Anyway, what does define your character is weather or not you are the type of person that can accept the challenge of change and do something about your problems in the future. With the instructions in this book I know you will do just that.

CHECK YOUR CREDIT REPORT

Checking your credit report is something that you should do often. I recommend a six-month check-up to ensure that there are no explainable blemishes or mistakes on your report.

There are small credit bureaus across the country and more than likely there is one in your area. Find your local credit bureau in the telephone book, then go in and ask for a copy of your credit report. There may or may not be a small fee for this but the fee is worth finding out where you stand.

Once you have received your credit report you may not be able to understand it. To someone that has never read a credit report it can be confusing and complicated. Ask someone at the credit bureau to explain it to you or take it to a loan officer at the bank and have him or her explain it to you.

That report should contain all the information a potential creditor would receive if you were applying for credit. If there are explainable blemishes on your credit such as being late with payments due to sickness, loss of job or divorce or if you find any mistakes on your credit report then you can write letters of explanation to the national credit bureaus.

Those letters of explanation will be included with you credit report and will be reflected at your local credit bureau. By doing this you will not erase the blemishes on your credit but the explanation may make them more understandable to someone that is checking your credit.

There are three major national credit bureaus. In order to obtain a free copy of your credit report from them or to explain blemishes, include your full name, address, social security and telephone numbers in a letter to the following addresses, attention consumer relations:

TRANS UNION
P.O. BOX 8070
NORTH OLMSTED, OHIO 44070

EQUIFAX
P.O. BOX 740193
ATLANTA, GEORGIA 30374

TRW CREDIT DATA
P.O. BOX 742827
DALLAS, TEXAS 75374

THE CREDIT STIMULATOR

After you have checked your credit, written letters of explanation for any blemishes and had any mistakes removed then you can use THE CREDIT STIMULATOR to vastly improve your credit in a short period of time.

Start a savings account at your local bank with the $100 per month extra that you have allocated for financial fitness. For the sake of example we will call this bank one. Put the $100 per month in bank one every month until you have accumulated $1000 dollars in your savings.

After you have accumulated $1000, call bank one and set up an appointment with a loan officer. On the day of your appointment make sure to dress up a bit and be very professional and business like. You will want to make a good impression because you are now working on developing a relationship with that bank.

When you arrive at the bank explain to the loan officer that you have $1000 in a savings account in bank one and that you would like to borrow $1000 using your savings account as collateral. Will you get the loan? Sure you will as long as the banks minimum loan amount is not over $1000. By ensuring payment to bank one with $1000 in a savings account at bank one, bank one will be more than happy to make the loan.

Have the payments set up for six months. Next take the $1000 that you borrowed from bank one and start a savings account at bank two. At bank two you will do the same thing that you did at bank one. Borrow $1000 using your savings as collateral.

Once again start a savings account this time at bank three with the $1000 you borrowed from bank two. Now you can borrow $1000 from bank three using once again a $1000 savings account. The final $1000 you can put into whichever account you choose. However do not spend the final $1000 or you will be incurring more debt.

At this point you will have three different $1000 loans at three different local banks that are to be paid in full at the end of six months. As soon as you receive the payment books in the mail immediately make a payment to all three banks.

After a week has passed make the second payments at all three banks. Wait another week and pay the third payments to all three banks. Already you have established that you are paying better than the terms that were agreed upon in your original loan agreement.

After making three payments you have the option to continue paying every week or to spread out the remaining three payments over the next three months.

I recommend that you spread them out over the next three months for two reasons. First, the bank is in business to make money and by paying a loan off in six weeks instead of six months then you drastically reduce the amount of money the bank makes from extending you a loan.

Secondly, by spreading out the remaining three payments over the next three months you will show a longer payment history. Regardless of how this is accomplished your credit as well as your standing with those three banks will be greatly improved. They will in fact say that you paid better than agreed upon.

- $1000 IN SAVINGS AT BANK ONE – BORROW $1000 FROM BANK ONE FOR SIX MONTHS USING SAVINGS AS COLLATERAL

- $1000 BORROWED FROM BANK ONE IN SAVINGS AT BANK TWO – BORROW $1000 FROM BANK TWO FOR SIX MONTHS USING SAVINGS AS COLLATERAL

- $1000 BORROWED FROM BANK TWO IN SAVINGS AT BANK THREE – BORROW $1000 FROM BANK THREE FOR SIX MONTHS USING SAVINGS AS COLLATERAL – PUT FINAL $1000 IN AN ACCOUNT FOR RE-PAYMENT

- MAKE WEEKLY PAYMENTS FOR FIRST THREE PAYMENTS – MAKE MONTHLY PAYMENTS FOR THE FINAL THREE PAYMENTS

After completing THE CREDIT STIMULATOR you will have obtained three local banks that like doing business with you at the small price of the interest that you paid for three six month loans.

From then on whenever you apply for credit you will be asked for credit references. Guess how many references are usually asked for? Yes, you guessed it, three. Three local banks will give you references saying that you pay better than you agreed.

Now back to the question of why you need good credit if you are planning on paying off your debts, not incurring anymore debts, and operating on a cash only basis. Remember when you learned about re-positioning your assets in chapter 5? You may be able to refinance your home using the equity to pay off high interest debts, reduce your monthly payments, and at the same time reduce your tax burdens. This was one of the **SMART** techniques that were covered in chapter 5.

Now imagine when it comes time to re-position your assets and the loan officer that is helping you refinance, checks your credit references. Do you think THE CREDIT STIMULATOR will have an effect on your approval or on the chance of getting a better interest rate? You bet it will.

Wow, there has been a lot of ground covered since you and I started this project. You now know how to get money working for you instead of against you. You have learned how to avoid a potential quarter of a million-dollar mistake, how not to be offended by the nine-letter dirty word, how to accumulate a lot of lagniappe along the way and finally how to bank on financial fitness.

We are nearing the end of the education process and soon you will learn how to apply all this information to your personal financial situation and everything will come together in full vivid perspective.

I hope that I have not rushed any of the subjects and lost you in the middle somewhere. Fortunately if you do not fully understand any of the things discussed you can always review or research other works on the subject. We live in the information age and there is literally tons of good information on this subject matter as well as others.

It has been my intention to give a panoramic view of personal finance in as short as time as possible in laymen terms. This is a subject that merits study and research but the main objective is to get started as soon as possible. Time is money.

I did say we were nearly done with the education process. There is still one chapter left before we begin applying financial fitness techniques. The next chapter is entitled RE-INVENTING THE WHEEL and for most of you it will be the hardest most challenging chapter of the entire book. For some it will be more difficult than finding an extra $100 per month.

RE-INVENTING THE WHEEL requires some work and discipline on your part. If you skip the next chapter and reason that you do not need it then you will lose to some degree later in life. If you accept the challenge then it will be a major asset in obtaining financial fitness as well as other goals in other areas of your life. So let's re-invent the wheel.

LIFE DOES NOT COME WITHOUT RISKS.
YOU LEARN TO TAKE THEM,
OR YOU STAY HOME AND WATCH LIFE ON TV.

JIMMY BUFFET

CHAPTER 8
RE-INVENTING THE WHEEL

Actually the title of this chapter should be re-inventing your life but you will be using a tool that is as useful as the wheel. Everyone makes use of the wheel but very few people make use of the tool that will be discussed in this chapter.

The people that do use this tool regularly become successful in their endeavors. This will be the hardest chapter in the entire book because it asks you to put forth some thought, some discipline, and some action. Nothing worthwhile comes without work and discipline so if you skip this chapter and think you do not need to do this then you will lose.

With that being said, the tool that will be discussed here is goal setting. Goal setting is making a list of what you want out of life, deciding which of those is most important to you, and developing a plan in order to obtain what it is that you desire.

To most people setting goals is a very laborious task and procrastination leads them down a road of broken dreams and unhappy days. No wonder there are so few people, who are wealthy and happy, it takes work.

If you are not clear on where it is that you want to go, and the actions that you need to take to get there, then how can you expect to arrive there? You don't have the wheels that you need to take you where you want to go.

Also you will have to develop discipline in order to overcome procrastination. It is possible to be busy and work hard all day and accomplish little or nothing. To look back on your day you may feel that you have worked hard so you must be making progress. Without a definite plan in writing of what you want to accomplish and how you plan to do it, you may not even realize that you are actually going in the opposite direction of your where you want to be.

For example if you want to put up $5.00 today in order to go toward your investment fund at the end of the month and you spend it instead. $5.00 does not seem like that big of a deal, and the day does not seem like that much of a failure, but when you figure a lifetime of those days they add up to make an unsuccessful life. On top of this you can figure in the compound interest that is not being paid on that $5.00 today.

Another example if you want to be debt-free and you go shopping with credit cards today, it may not seem like such a big deal. After all you have been incurring debt all your life and you are not in that bad of shape. This will add up not only in debt but also in negative interest that is working against you to destroy your dream of financial fitness.

By committing your goals to paper and constantly working and revising them, you will find that you will have fewer unsuccessful days. You will realize how devastating to your overall plan incurring debt and not saving $5.00 today will be.

You give your life purpose when you reduce goals to paper. Yet goal setting is not just for business or financial goals. You can set goals for every facet of your life. If you feel that you are not smart set goals on educating yourself. If you are not happy, start a happiness plan. Of course if you are not rich, set goals that will make you rich. You do not have to be rich in order to have a rich plan.

Do however keep in mind that you will not accomplish every goal that you set. Some of them may require more sacrifice from you than you are willing to give. Some you may decide after you have pursued them awhile that it is not what you really want after all. Still setting goals can help you accomplish virtually anything that you want to accomplish in life.

Just for example, you will learn in the remainder of this writing how to set financial goals, if you get that even half way right you will improve the quality of your life. Because of the subject matter of this book I will only deal with financial goal setting but do not limit yourself with this tool.

As far as financial goal setting goes, it does not matter where you are at financially. That is immaterial at this time and does not reflect on you as a human being. You can be a decent hard working American and still end up in bankruptcy. It happens all the time. The important thing is that you start somewhere.

Develop a plan, commit it to paper, and take action in order to accomplish your goal. All three of those steps are as important as the other one. Do not set goals in your head, or leave them lying around to gather dust with no action taken on them. Setting goals is actually a lifestyle that comes with the habit of practicing it. Here now is the best that I have learned on setting goals. Take this tool and use it, for just like the wheel it will take you where you want to go.

THE WISH LIST

Some people call this a dream list but no matter what you decide to call it, it is a list of the things that you want from life. The things you want to do the places you want to visit, and the things that you want to become.

While making this list imagine that you are not limited in anyway by time, money or ability. This list is actually what you have always wished for yourself and what you have dreamed of. Imagine for awhile that you have a Genie's lamp and your Genie has granted you an unlimited amount of wishes. What would you wish for? Get it on paper.

Spend twenty to thirty minutes somewhere that you will not be disturbed and make out your wish list. On the following page you will find a sheet that you can use to make out your wish list. Write fast and abbreviate, this is not a time to go into detail, just get your ideas down. Keep writing until you have twenty-five to fifty wishes on your list.

Keep writing until you have twenty-five to fifty wishes on your list. You can add to this list anytime that something pops into your mind. For example if you are watching TV and a documentary comes on about treasure hunting and it fascinates you and you wish you could do it, write it on your wish list.

MY WISH LIST

DATE:_____-_____-_____

_____
(YOUR NAME)

___1 _____
___2 _____
___3 _____
___4 _____
___5 _____
___6 _____
___7 _____
___8 _____
___9 _____
___10 _____
___11 _____
___12 _____
___13 _____
___14 _____
___15 _____
___16 _____
___17 _____
___18 _____
___19 _____
___20 _____
___21 _____
___22 _____
___23 _____
___24 _____
___25 _____
___26 _____
___27 _____
___28 _____
___29 _____
___30 _____
___31 _____
___32 _____
___33 _____
___34 _____
___35 _____
___36 _____
___37 _____
___38 _____
___39 _____
___40 _____

CATEGORIZE EACH WISH

Out to the side of each wish put a number that represents how long that you believe it will take to accomplish this goal. If you believe it will take you a year put a one by it. If you think it will take five years then put a five by it and of course put a ten by the ones that you believe will take you ten years to accomplish.

PICK THE FIVE MOST IMPORTANT WISHES

Here you must spend a little time analyzing not only what it is that you want but also why you want it. Some goals are set entirely for wealth. Wealth however may not appeal to you as much as personal satisfaction or peace of mind or acceptance of your peers or spouse.

It is critical for you to know what you want from life but it is equally important for you to know why you want it. If you have set a goal and the reason that you have set it is unclear or it does not agree with what is most important to you then you may actually sabotage yourself on accomplishing this goal.

It is important to write out a purpose statement when you pick a wish to become a goal in order to make it clear why you want that particular wish. So spend some time analyzing why you want to accomplish this goal. This is where you talk yourself into going for it or decide that it is not worth the sacrifice required.

Once you have decided that a wish is worthy of becoming a goal you should add it to a separate goal sheet that you can see and read at least twice per day. Because of people being jealous of your attempts to better yourself it is a good policy to keep your goals to yourself. Don't forget that misery loves company so if your friends and family are not doing well you may be ridiculed and discouraged. Remember everyone has opinions but very few have workable plans of action.

CREATE A JOURNAL

Inside your journal you should keep a copy of your wish list, the statements of your five most important goals and the plans of actions that you will begin to build in order to accomplish your goals.

I would recommend a 9 ½ x 6-inch three to five subject notebook for your journal because of the space and convenience.

CREATE A DEFINITE PLAN OF ACTION

Your plan of action for each goal should contain the name of the goal, the date you begin, the date you plan to complete the goal, a statement of your purpose, the steps that you feel you need to take in order to accomplish that goal, and a completion date. This will serve as a road map to an end that you have designated.

At this point you may not really know the exact steps that you need to take but the knowledge will come as you begin to research how to accomplish your goal. The important part is to begin; you can edit your plans, as information becomes available to you. For now just put down the 3 to 6 most important things that you believe that you will have to complete in order to accomplish your goal. Each step that you complete will be another rung on the ladder that leads to success.

By the time that you accomplish each step on your plan of action you should have accomplished your goal. If you have not then research what you hope to accomplish some more and add additional steps and continue to work towards their accomplishment.

After you have a definite written plan of action then all you have to do is follow the plan. Be sure that each step toward the end is actually a goal itself. This will give you rewards and confidence as you accomplish each step.

Now I went through this process of goal setting fairly quickly with general descriptions on how it works. You might be a little undecided as to how you want to go about setting up your own personal system for setting goals. Do not worry just yet because I am going to go through the process with you step by step and help you develop a financial fitness set of goals. I will give you specific examples and you choose the ones that apply to your needs.

The best teacher is experience and you will get that experience here. I have taken workshops on setting goals, attended several seminars and read books on the subject. In my opinion there is a certain amount of over kill.

Setting goals and working your plan is of utmost importance but do not get so involved in creating your plan that you never have time to work it. You will want to have the KISS rule working here, which means Keep It Simple Stupid.

It is no wonder that most people do not set and work goals. When it is taught it usually is taught in such a way that it seems like a lot of work.

Set your goals, commit them to writing, and start taking action at once. If something does not work then re-think, and re-organize your plan, but do not spend all your time on planning.

Spend minimum time planning and maximum time working. So I have shown very basically how to set and work goals for the reason of simplicity. Now it is time to take everything that you have learned and start applying it.

Most of the remainder of this book will be in the format of plans of action. These are step by step instructions for your paycheck in order for you to end up where I think everyone would like to be; financial fitness. I believe that should be everyone's number one goal for several reasons.

Financial fitness will greatly improve the quality of your life, because without financial worries you can concentrate your energy on other more important things in your life. Love and family being two things that are more important than money.

The second reason is that if you are financially fit you can actually help others who are less fortunate than yourself and that creates a sense of purpose in life.

The final reason is the sense of accomplishment of becoming the person that it took to become in order to have financial fitness. I am challenging you to treat yourself and your life like a business. Most people work harder for their employer than they do for themselves. Some of you do required paperwork, reports, payroll and other laborious tasks at your jobs but you will not sit down and write out your goals.

You are the business and your goals are your products and they will be worth more to you than the wage you receive from your employer.

However by designing your life and working toward worthwhile goals you will become more content, more confident and it will show in your life overall and you will mostly probably find yourself doing a better job for your employer as well. You will in fact be respected and admired.

So without further adieu let's get busy getting financially fit.

SCHOOL IS OUT! GO TO WORK!

THE OFFICIAL INSTRUCTION BOOK FOR
YOUR PAYCHECK

I AM THE MASTER OF MY FATE,
I AM THE CAPTAIN OF MY SOUL.

HENLEY

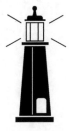

CHAPTER 9
YOUR WISH IS MY COMMAND

There is a very simple formula to achieve what it is that you want from life. The formula is ask. Actually the entire formula is ask and you shall receive. It is important to note that it does not say whine, bitch and moan and you shall receive.

I have up until this point tried to write this book without a religious overtone however there are things taught in the Bible that just can not be ignored. This is a powerful formula and it is taught in the Bible.

The problem with the formula is that people do not know how to ask properly. The very first thing that you have to learn about asking is how to ask specifically. You should have already made a wish list at this point. The wish list is a very general description of what it is that you want. The next step is to transfer that wish to your goal list and at that time you should go into detail.

For example you may have on your wish list a car, but by the time it makes it to your goal list it should read a black 1963 Cadillac, fully restored with the engine chromed and a picture of Hank Williams airbrushed on the hood. I will have fur dice hanging on the mirror, the windows will be tinted and I will have one of the old gas pedals that look like a foot. I will have a tag on the front of this car black and silver that reads "Drifter".

In other words go into as much detail as possible in order to paint a vivid picture of exactly what it is that you want. After you have a clear mental picture of what it is that you want and have committed it to paper that is a way of asking for what you want.

The next thing that you should know about asking is how to do it with faith. In other words believe that you can accomplish this goal just as a child believes that they can do anything they want to do.

Of course asking involves some intelligence also. You have to ask the right person. You would not ask a doctor on advice about re-building the motor in your 1963 Cadillac unless that doctor's past time is working on classic cars. So ask someone who can help you and of course you will have to give something in return. Nothing is free. If you ask someone to help you make sure that first you have something of value to offer to him or her in return.

The final step in asking is to ask until you receive the object of your desire. So many people give up on their hopes and dreams just before they would have accomplished them had they kept on trying. Remember that delays are not denials.

Matthew chapter 7 verse 7 is where the Bible says "Ask and it shall be given you" but it does not stop there. It also says "Seek, and you shall find; knock and it shall be opened unto you". In other words asking is just a portion of the formula; you have to work for it.

As I stated written goals are a way of asking from yourself what you want to accomplish but you must also take some action on those written goals. When you research what it will take for you to accomplish a goal then you are seeking. When you begin to take the steps that you have outlined in your plans then you are knocking at the door of opportunity.

If you only ask and do not take the actions of seeking and knocking then you will have a goal list that will never be accomplished.

Matthew chapter 7 verse 8 goes on to say "For everyone that asks receives: and he that seeks, finds: and to him that knocks it shall be opened. Your abilities will grow as you learn to ask, seek, and knock.

While we are on the subject of the Bible I am sure that you have heard it said, "Money is the root of all evil" which is actually misquoted. The Bible says in I Timothy 6:10 "For the **love** of money is the root of all evil". In other words there is nothing wrong with being successful and wealthy as long as that is not the most important thing in your life.

As a matter of a fact the entire book of Proverbs teaches how to become wealthy and successful in life. You do not have to feel guilty about being successful.

However money will only serve to make you more of what you already are. If you are miserable and unhappy in life then more money will make you even more miserable. If you indulge in say for example alcohol and you obtain a fortune, now you can afford to become a drunk. The secret to becoming wealthy is to be happy with where you are at in life before it comes along so that it will increase your happiness instead of increasing your misery.

The accumulation of money is not a need but a want. According to the book of Matthew we are all promised our needs to be provided by our heavenly father even more so than our earthly father would provide. Do not spend your time being depressed about financial matters. You are very much alive and your basic needs will be provided for. Consider this fact, if you are having trouble paying your bills, then what can they do to you? Sure they can sue you and make your life miserable but they can not kill you just because you can not pay your bills. You are okay alive and well so get off the pity party and learn to help yourself.

The Bible teaches us to believe and have faith and that is exactly what you must do in order to make anything happen. The Bible or this book or any other book can not help you unless you are willing to help yourself.

The Bible also says, "Where there is no vision the people perish" Proverbs 29:18. Setting goals is actually your vision of what you want the future to hold for you and without it you will be unsuccessful in one degree or another. I have already stated before that money is not everything and should not be your driving force in life but actually a means to improve the quality of your life.

The Bible is not the only book that talks about asking and receiving. The following is a poem quoted from a book entitled THINK AND GROW RICH if you have not read this book then I recommend you do so as soon as possible.

I BARGAINED WITH LIFE FOR A PENNY,
  AND LIFE WOULD PAY NO MORE,
HOWEVER I BEGGED AT EVENING
  WHEN I COUNTED MY SCANTY STORE.

FOR LIFE IS A JUST EMPLOYER,
  HE GIVES YOU WHAT YOU ASK,
BUT ONCE YOU HAVE SET THE WAGES,
  WHY, YOU MUST BEAR THE TASK.

I WORKED FOR A MENIAL'S HIRE,
  ONLY TO LEARN, DISMAYED,
THAT ANY WAGE I HAD ASKED OF LIFE,
  LIFE WOULD HAVE WILLINGLY PAID.

THINK AND GROW RICH
NAPOLEON HILL

MATTHEW 6: 25-30

25- THEREFORE I SAY UNTO YOU, TAKE NO THOUGHT FOR YOUR LIFE, WHAT YE SHALL EAT, OR WHAT YE SHALL DRINK; NOR YET FOR YOUR BODY, WHAT YE SHALL PUT ON. IS NOT THE LIFE MORE THAN MEAT, AND THE BODY THAN RAIMENT?

26- BEHOLD THE FOWLS OF THE AIR: FOR THEY SOW NOT, NEITHER DO THEY REAP, NOR GATHER INTO BARNS; YET YOUR HEAVENLY FATHER FEEDETH THEM. ARE YE NOT MUCH BETTER THAN THEY?

27- WHICH OF YOU BY TAKING THOUGHT CAN ADD ONE CUBIT UNTO HIS STATURE?

28- AND WHY TAKE YE THOUGHT FOR RAIMENT? CONSIDER THE LILIES OF THE FIELD, HOW THEY GROW; THEY TOIL NOT, NEITHER DO THEY SPIN:

29- AND YET I SAY UNTO YOU, THAT EVEN SOLOMON IN ALL HIS GLORY WAS NOT ARRAYED LIKE ONE OF THESE.

30- WHEREFORE, IF GOD SO CLOTHE THE GRASS OF THE FIELD, WHICH TODAY IS, AND TOMORROW IS CAST INTO THE OVEN, SHALL HE NOT MUCH MORE CLOTHE YOU, O YE OF LITTLE FAITH?

MATTHEW 7: 7-11

7- ASK, AND IT SHALL BE GIVEN YOU; SEEK, AND YE SHALL FIND; KNOCK, AND IT SHALL BE OPENED UNTO YOU.

8- FOR EVERYONE THAT ASKETH, RECEIVETH: AND HE THAT SEEKETH, FINDETH: AND TO HIM THAT KNOCKETH IT SHALL BE OPENED.

9- OR WHAT MAN IS THERE OF YOU, WHOM IF HIS SON ASK BREAD, WILL HE GIVE HIM A STONE?

10- OR IF HE ASK A FISH, WILL HE GIVE HIM A SERPENT?

11- IF YE THEN BEING EVIL KNOW HOW TO GIVE GOOD GIFTS UNTO YOUR CHILDREN, HOW MUCH MORE SHALL YOUR FATHER WHICH IS IN HEAVEN GIVE GOOD GIFTS TO THEM THAT ASK HIM?

You have finally arrived at the "meat and potatoes" of Financial Fitness. It is time to apply what you have learned to your own unique financial situation. In the next few pages you will be given specific plans and will see first hand how to use them. The first order of business is to write out a mission statement of what you hope to accomplish by setting and working your goals.

THE MISSION STATEMENT

This is the part where you write out the reasons why this goal is important to you and why it will benefit you. You will examine if this goal is actually something that you want to put quality time and effort into. This mission statement should be done for every goal for two reasons.

The number one reason is to make sure that you are totally committed to achieving your goal and it agrees with your overall plan. Next is the subconscious effect that it will have. In other words you should read your mission statement everyday and review your plans of actions in order to feed it to your subconscious mind.

Your subconscious mind will actually take the information and help you find ways to create a plan to produce the desired effect, which is the attainment of your goal.

Now it is time to create a mission statement for your financial fitness plan and go through the instructions to get you there. On page 102 you will find a sample mission statement. You can either use it as is or create one in your own words.

You will notice that there is a place for both you and your spouse's signature. If you are married then you are in a partnership and you have to do this together. I am assuming that by you reading this that you are the primary breadwinner and decision-maker in your household.

If that is the case then you are the business, goals are the product and your spouse is your partner in the business of you. You can not expect to achieve financial fitness with any degree of success without the loving co-operation from your partner. Share these plans with your partner and the results will be multiplied.

All of this I say using the voice of experience once again. I am not qualified to be a marriage counselor but I have been in a marriage that was a total disaster and now I currently enjoy a good marriage. It is a much better experience when you have a partner that will work with you.

You will find that the co-operation from your spouse will serve as a catalyst to accomplishing your goals and you will be more confident that you can accomplish anything.

Again I believe that financial fitness is a goal that everyone should be interested in achieving and I am equally sure that is the reason you have put forth the time and money with this book. Be persistent and you will reap the benefits. Have faith and concentrate on working your plan until it is accomplished.

FINANCIAL FITNESS MISSION STATEMENT

DATE: ___-___-___

I KNOW THAT I HAVE THE ABILITY TO BECOME FINANCIALLY FIT AND I HERE AND NOW PROMISE TO TAKE THE ACTIONS NECESSARY TO ACHIEVING THIS GOAL. I WILL BECOME COMPLETELY DEBT-FREE AND OPERATE ON A CASH ONLY BASIS IN ORDER TO IMPROVE THE QUALITY OF MINE AND MY FAMILY'S LIFE. I FULLY UNDERSTAND THAT THIS UNDERTAKING WILL TAKE TIME AND PERSISTENCE AND I HERE AND NOW PROMISE TO RENDER THE ACTION NECESSARY TO ACCOMPLISH THIS GOAL. I WILL SUCCEED IN THIS ENDEAVOR BECAUSE I HAVE CLEARLY WRITTEN PLANS OF ACTIONS AND I WILL FOLLOW THESE PLANS NO MATTER HOW LONG IT TAKES TO THE END THAT I AM SEEKING.

X_____
    (YOUR SIGNATURE)

X_____
    (SPOUSE'S SIGNATURE)

FIND OUT WHERE YOU ARE

In order for you to achieve any goal you must first have a starting point. Knowing where you are at financially is of utmost importance even before you decide where you want to go. You have to have a way to measure and monitor your progress so the next step is to be aware of where you are.

There are several tools that you will be using for just that purpose and there are worksheets provided in order to help you gather the information you need to find your starting point.

PREPARE A FINANCIAL STATEMENT

Preparing a financial statement is the first place that you will start in your analysis of where you are. On page 105 you will find a worksheet for figuring your net worth. Net worth is nothing more than what you own (your assets) minus what you owe (your liabilities) and the resulting information is your financial statement.

A financial statement can be very intimidating; you may find yourself with a lot more liabilities than you have assets. The first financial statement I completed left me feeling embarrassed. Do not fret while you are doing this. It is a financial statement and as I have stated before on numerous occasions, it has no bearing on you as a person.

Besides, a financial statement should be done every six months. By the time that you have completed your second financial statement you will have assets where you once had liabilities and a warm feeling of accomplishment will replace the inadequate feelings of the first.

TRACK YOUR SPENDING

On the pages following the financial statement worksheet, you will find two other worksheets that will be useful in tracking your spending and creating a budget. The first of those documents is entitled Spending Record and the second one is labeled Bills. The spending record is for you to tally up what you have spent and what it was for on a weekly basis.

The spending record enclosed is my own personal record so you will probably need to add some categories of your own or make changes to the ones already listed.

In order to complete the spending record you will need to obtain two pocket size notepads. One notepad for yourself and one for your spouse.

Pick a day, the first of the month is a good time to start. From that day forward for at least three months record in your notepad everything that you spend to the penny and what it was for.

CREATE A BUDGET

After three months of recording your spending you will have two key pieces of information. Number one will be a total of how much you need each month for each category. You can then use the spending record to list and work your budget in the future.

The second key piece of information that you will obtain is the recognition of the categories that you compulsively over spend on. This will allow you to plan for the reduction of spending on those categories by using your budget. You will in fact begin to find a little lagniappe that you can apply to your investment goals instead of wasting.

Finding that lagniappe will be up to you. You will have to decide how much is too much to spend on any one category and you will also have to make the sacrifices in order to change that amount.

As far as the record sheet entitled Bills goes you will use it everytime a bill comes in your mailbox. This worksheet will allow you to keep up, with which bills have and have not been paid for the month, and what your balance is on each. You should never again lose, or forget to pay a bill because the information will all be together in one place at your fingertips and all you have to do is mark a **X** by the bills when they are paid.

At a glance you will also see how you are progressing toward financial fitness. To start with you will notice very little difference in your Bills document from month to month. At some point however as your assets begin to grow and your liabilities begin to diminish you will start to notice a drastic change.

FINANCIAL STATEMENT WORK SHEET

SHORT TERM ASSETS

$_____CASH
$_____SAVINGS ACCOUNT BALANCES
$_____CHECKING ACCOUNT BALANCES
$_____MONEY MARKET ACCOUNTS
$_____EMERGENCY FUNDS
$_____CD'S OR OTHER SAVINGS
$_____CASH VALUES

LONG TERM ASSETS

$_____MUTUAL FUNDS
$_____IRA'S
$_____OTHER RETIREMENT FUNDS
$_____STOCKS
$_____BONDS
$_____RESIDENTIAL REAL ESTATE
$_____INVESTMENT REAL ESTATE
$_____OTHER LONG TERM INVESTMENTS

PERSONAL PROPERTY

$_____ TOOLS AND EQUIPMENT
$_____AUTOMOBILES
$_____COLLECTIBLES
$_____OTHER PERSONAL PROPERTY

$_____TOTAL ASSETS

LIABILITIES

$_____MORTGAGES
$_____NOTES
$_____AUTO LOANS
$_____CREDIT CARDS
$_____OTHER LIABILITIES

$_____TOTAL LIABILITIES

$_____ MINUS $_____ EQUALS $_____
        ASSETS   LIABILITIES   NET WORTH

SPENDING RECORD-MONTH OF _____ 20 _____

WEEK	1	2	3	4	5	TOTAL
BEAUTY SALON						
BEER						
BOOKS						
CAT						
CHARITY						
CHILD						
CIGARETTES						
CLOTHES						
CREDIT CARDS						
COSMETICS						
DINERS/FAST FOOD						
DRINKS/ SNACKS						
EDUCATION						
ELECTRICITY						
ENTERTAIN.						
FURNISHINGS						
GIFTS						
GROC.						
HOBBIES						
HOME EQUIP.						
HOME REPAIR/MORT						
HOME SUPPLIES						
INVESTMENTS						
JEWELRY						
LIFE INS.						
MAGAZINES						
MEDICAL						
OFFICE SUPPLIES						
PERSONAL DEBT						
PERSONAL CARE						
PERSONAL GROWTH						
PHONE						
PRO. DUES						
SONGS						
TIPS						
TRUCK						
SALES TAX						
TOTAL						

BILLS FOR MONTH OF: _____ 20__

X	COMPANY/DESCRIPTION	PAYMENT	DATE DUE	DATE PAID	CHECK #	BALANCE

BALANCE YOUR CHECKING ACCOUNT

If you have made it this far toward financial fitness without giving up then congratulations. Humans resist change but change is the only way to correct any problem. I fully realize that I am asking for a lot of time, effort and paperwork from you. That's what it takes in order to build the business of you.

Here we have arrived at another one of those difficult tasks for most people, balancing your checking account. To a lot of people this subject ranks right up there with programming the VCR remote; we don't understand and we don't want to learn.

Nevertheless, it is a must to learn how to balance your checking account in order to arrive at financial fitness. It only takes a few minutes per month and it will save you from having to pay lagniappe to the bank in the form of NSF charges. The bank makes enough money from investing other people's money, do not give them anymore.

Balancing your checking account may even provide you with some lagniappe. My wife and I for a long time were not balancing our checking account for the very same reason that most people don't, we just never got around to it. My wife in order to avoid being over drawn would round our deposits off and not count the change in our register. On top of that at times when we made small deposits she would not add them either.

Imagine our surprise when we did finally balance our checking account and found several hundred dollars worth of lagniappe that we had no idea was there. We might have never known we had that money had we not taking the time to balance our account.

If you are serious about financial fitness, take the time to balance your account. On the next page you will find a worksheet that will help take some of the mystery out of the process. You should receive a similar worksheet with your monthly statement however should you need to make copies of the worksheet, please feel free to do so.

If you are having trouble balancing your account, there are a couple of things that you can do. You can stop making deposits and stop writing checks and use cash only for a month until you know exactly what your balance is.

Or you can take your information to the bank and they will help you reconcile it for free. Whatever you do get it balanced and keep it balanced, it will serve you well.

CHECKING ACCOUNT BALANCE SHEET:

Outstanding Checks-Have Not Yet Went Through

CHECK NUMBER	AMOUNT				
#			ENTER STATEMENT BALANCE	$	
			ADD DEPOSITS NOT YET CREDITED		
			TOTAL		
			SUBTRACT TOTAL OF OUTSTANDING CHECKS		
			THIS SHOULD EQUAL YOUR CHECKBOOK BALANCE		
			SUBTRACT MONTHLY SERVICE CHARGE		
			SUBTRACT ANY OTHER FEES THAT APPEAR ON YOUR STATEMENT		
			NEW BALANCE FOR REGISTER		
TOTAL	$				

-Sort your checks by number
-Check off in your register each check that has been paid by the bank
-List check # and amount of checks not yet paid in the space provided
-Use the space above to reconcile your statement-If the balance that states "this should equal your checkbook balance" does not equal your checkbook balance then re-check your account. If it is still not the same contact your bank immediately.

FINANCIAL FITNESS PLAN OF ACTION #1: OBTAIN A VIVID PICTURE OF WHERE WE ARE AT FINANCIALLY.

START DATE: ___-___-___ PLANNED COMPLETION DATE: ___-___-___

PURPOSE: In order to obtain financial fitness we must find out where we are at financially and how we got to this point. We will take the necessary steps outlined in this plan to gather that information.

_____**STEP 1:** Prepare and sign a written mission statement in order to commit to a plan of action towards financial fitness.

_____**STEP 2:** Prepare a financial statement that reflects our net worth. Furthermore we will commit to completing a financial statement every six months.

_____**STEP 3:** Obtain two pocket size spiral bound notebooks one each for me and my spouse along with a pen that will easily be kept on our persons at all times. Starting ____-____-____ we will keep a written record to the penny of everything that we spend for 3 months and write it down in our notebooks. We will also keep receipts on everything that we spend.

_____**STEP 4:** We will keep a record of our spending for at least 3 months categorizing our spending at the end of each month so that we can plan a budget with no surprises. We will create a budget from this information and will commit to a budget on a monthly basis.

_____**STEP 5:** Keep track of our bills on a monthly basis on a bill sheet so that we will not miss a payment and we can watch our liabilities decrease.

_____**STEP 6:** We will learn to balance our checking account and will do so every month as soon as it arrives and use this also as a written record as to what we spend.

COMPLETION DATE: ___-___-___

FINANCIAL FITNESS PLAN OF ACTION #2: AVOID THE QUARTER OF A MILLION-DOLLAR MISTAKE.

START DATE: ___-___-___ **PLANNED COMPLETION DATE:** ___-___-___

PURPOSE: To take control of our money and reap the benefits from the interest instead of allowing someone else control.

_____**STEP 1:** Re-read chapter 3 AVOIDING THE QUARTER OF A MILLION-DOLLAR MISTAKE. Research, obtain prospectuses and decide on a good quality growth mutual fund.

_____**STEP 2:** Set up a 401k account at our place of employment immediately and commit 5-10% of gross income to be taken out in payroll deductions for this account.

_____**STEP 3:** Transfer any savings accounts other than emergency funds into the decided upon growth mutual fund. Set mutual fund up as an IRA in order to reduce taxes. Invest any lagniappe accumulated in plan of action #1 into this account.

_____**STEP 4:** Commit an additional $30 per month (only $1 per day) to decided upon mutual fund in a systematic investment

_____**STEP 5:** Re-read chapter 4, THE NINE LETTER DIRTY WORD and THE NINE-LETTER DIRTY WORD RE-VISITED in chapter 5 determine the basic amount of life insurance that we need.

$_____ X 8 = Basic amount of coverage
  (Your annual income)

$_____ x 8 = Basic amount of coverage
  (spouse's annual income)

   Children should be included on your policy as a rider in order to save policies fees. Only purchase enough insurance on your children in order to bury them. They are not the breadwinners so only about $10,000 coverage is needed.

_____**STEP 6:** Obtain quotes on Term life insurance and replace any Cash-value life insurance or credit life insurance that we own according to THE RULES OF BUY TERM AND INVEST THE DIFFERENCE set forth in chapter 4.

_____**STEP 7:** Put existing cash value into a mutual fund and begin investing the difference in the cost of the Term and Cash-value into our mutual fund.

_____**STEP 8:** Re-read UNCLE SAM IS NOT SANTA CLAUSE in chapter 5 and lower our tax amount if we are paying in too much. We will put the extra bring home pay into an interest bearing account.

_____**STEP 9:** when we have sufficient funds in an emergency fund we will raise the deductibles on our other insurance programs and invest the savings of premium.

COMPLETION DATE: ___-___-___

FINANCIAL FITNESS PLAN OF ACTION #3: OPERATE ON A CASH ONLY BASIS.

START DATE: ___-___-___ **PLANNED COMPLETION DATE:** ___-___-___

PURPOSE: In order to become completely debt-free, we must learn how to operate on a cash only basis. This will enable us to avoid using credit cards and other debt. If we have cash we do not need credit.

_____STEP 1: Accumulate $1000 in pocket money. $500 for both my spouse and I. We will commit $_____ per month that we have allocated in extra money in order to realize this goal. When we have accumulated this money we will use it to make purchases instead of credit and then build the cash back up before we make any additional purchases.
   The following amounts represent the denominations that we plan to have in cash money on our persons at all time and we will never carry less:

My $500 pocket money # of bills	Spouse's $500 pocket money # of bills
___$100 bills	___$100 bills
___$50 bills	___$50 bills
___$20 bills	___$20 bills
___$10 bills	___$10 bills
___$5 bills	___$5 bills
___$1 bills	___$1 bills

_____STEP 2: We will remove all credit cards from our persons and put in a box at home. We will learn not to use credit anymore.

COMPLETION DATE: ____-____-____

There are a couple of other reasons for having cash on you at all times. The first reason being the sense of security it brings. Just by putting the first $500 that you make into your pocket you feel great, like you have accomplished something. Not only that but it can also save you from some embarrassing situations.

I am sure that you have experienced a time when you needed a couple of dollars for something and were embarrassed because you did not have it. Maybe you had to borrow a few dollars from someone and felt embarrassed asking for the money. Now you will no longer have that feeling of embarrassment. Carrying a few hundred dollars will make sure that you never have to be in that situation again.

Still if you carry heavy and do not learn how to control your spending habits and are still incurring debt then you are not getting anywhere. Soon your $500 will be gone and you will be broke and unhappy.

It may take you a little time to accumulate $500 a piece especially if you are only using $100 per month to do this plan. That does not matter, the important thing is that you set a date to have the money, accumulate it and move on to your next goal.

If for some reason you are uncomfortable with carrying large sums of money with you then you can always put the money in savings or checking and obtain an ATM/debit card in order to have this money at your disposal. However you do it is up to you, just make sure that you accumulate the required sums of money and wean yourself off the credit cards.

I have heard all the excuses why you will have to keep at least one credit card with you. Everything from "What if an emergency comes up?" to "I may need to rent a car."

The fact is that you do not need a credit card period. I was nearly 30 years old before I obtained my first credit card and I survived just fine without one. I do not carry credit cards now and I constantly travel. You must make the commitment to stay away from the credit cards. If you must have a piece of plastic then do as I said and obtain an ATM/debit card.

An ATM/debit card will do for you anything that a credit card will except for get you in debt. When you run out of money you can't use your card but you will not have to pay interest on your purchases either.

You will notice that I have not asked you to cut up your credit cards, not yet anyway. I have noticed that most people resist doing this because they feel like they are losing something.

You will have to cut up the cards when the time comes but your purpose here is to learn how to get along without them. You can do that with the security of knowing they are in tact in a box at home and that will put less pressure on you for the time being.

FINANCIAL FITNESS PLAN OF ACTION #4 THE CREDIT STIMULATOR

START DATE: ___-___-___ **PLANNED COMPLETION DATE:** ___-___-___

PURPOSE: To improve our credit in a short period of time and improve our relationship with the bank.

_____**STEP 1:** Re-read chapter 7 BANKING ON FINANCIAL FITNESS.

_____**STEP 2:** Obtain a copy of our credit report and learn how to read it. We will commit to checking our credit once every six months.

_____**STEP 3:** Write letters of explanations for any explainable blemishes and have any mistakes removed.

_____**STEP 4:** We will accumulate $1000 by using our $_____ per month commitment and we will have the money by _____-_____-_____

_____**STEP 5:** Using the $1000 we have accumulated we will obtain and pay off 3 $1000 loans at 3 different banks according to the techniques set forth in THE CREDIT STIMULATOR.

COMPLETION DATE: ___-___-___

FINANCIAL FITNESS PLAN OF ACTION #5: RE- POSITION OUR ASSETS

NOTE: If you are not a homeowner, do not have enough equity to pay off all unsecured debt, or are unable to get re-financing at a decent rate because of credit problems then complete steps 1, 2, and 4 then proceed to the next plan of action.

START DATE: ___-___-___ **PLANNED COMPLETION DATE:** ___-___-___

PURPOSE: To lower the interest we are paying on unsecured debt by using the equity in our home to pay them off. We will also reduce our monthly payments and save money in taxes.

_____**STEP 1:** Re-read chapter 5 A LITTLE LAGNIAPPE

_____**STEP 2:** Call each credit company and ask for a lower interest rate. We may not get it but if we don't ask then we won't receive.

_____**STEP 3:** Apply for and obtain a home equity line of credit in order to pay off as many of the unsecured debts as possible. Do so according to the techniques described in chapter 5.

_____**STEP 4:** We will retain a lawyer at this time to help us refinance our home (for those refinancing) and to have a Will drawn up.

_____**STEP 5:** We will close out the accounts, cut up all credit cards that are paid off through our equity and commit to not incurring any additional debt. Furthermore we will not spend the savings per month but use it to continue paying off existing debt.

COMPLETION DATE: ___-___-___

FINANCIAL FITNESS PLAN OF ACTION #6: ELIMINATE DEBT

PURPOSE: To become completely debt free and have a better more enjoyable quality of life.

_____**STEP 1:** We will use the techniques described in THE MORTGAGE ACCELERATOR in order to make at least one extra payment per year on our mortgage.

_____**STEP 2:** Using the $_____ commitment per month we will continue to pay off our unsecured by using the techniques described in THE DEBT ELIMINATOR.

_____**STEP 3:** We will continue to close out accounts and cut up credit cards as they are paid off and further commit to not incurring any additional debt.

_____**STEP 4:** After all unsecured debt is paid in full we will commit the money that we were paying for unsecured debts to a plan for becoming financially independent.

COMPLETION DATE: ___-___-___

During the last steps you have found that it is time to cut up your credit cards. I have a small, clear plastic jar that sits on my desk and contains my cut up credit cards. Even as I look at it now it gives me a sense of pride and accomplishment. The chains of a debt prison from the past now sit harmlessly cut up in a jar.

In order for me to remain completely honest, my wife and I did not cut up every credit card we owned. We still have a couple but we did not use them until we were in the position to pay off the full balance every month. You may decide to keep a credit card or two and I can not stop you. If however you can not pay it off in full every month then get rid of it, it will only put you back where you were before you worked so hard to get where you are at. I do recommend if you keep some accounts open that you not carry the cards with you until you are absolutely confident that you have learned not to depend on debt.

In the last step you will notice that you will have all unsecured debt paid. The only thing that you should be left owing is your mortgage. There are now options where before there were liabilities. When you have completed all those steps you will have in fact achieved FINANCIAL FITNESS. So what do you do with all the money you have freed up every month from paying off all that unsecured debt?

You may want to pay all that money towards your mortgage but eventually it will be paid in full and the question remains, what do I do now? Should you invest all that extra money into a mutual fund?

The answer is no. The last step reads that you should commit all that extra money towards a plan for becoming financially independent. Financial independence is achieved when you do not have to work anymore and you have enough money to enjoy your life. Investing in mutual funds will be part of becoming financially independent but it is not the entire answer.

It will take you some time but eventually you will complete all the steps set forth in your pursuit of financial fitness. Once you have completed those steps then congratulations will be in order. You will be in a position that few people ever know and that is financial fitness.

My job is done; I have accomplished what I set out to do. However I am not going to leave you with unanswered questions. If you are unsure where to go from here you may just decide to spend all the money and live it up for as long as you can.

Once you have accomplished one goal you must have another one to pursue. If there is nothing left to accomplish then life has no purpose.

Therefore another chapter is in order. I can't just leave you hanging with no plan for financial independence. Chapter 10 is entitled FROM FITNESS TO INDEPENDENCE and it covers ideas for helping you become financially independent.

WHEN WE ARE BORN, WE CRY AND THE WORLD REJOICES.
LIVE YOUR LIFE SO THAT WHEN YOU DIE YOU WILL REJOICE AND
THE WORLD WILL CRY.

ANCIENT INDIAN PROVERB

CHAPTER 10
FROM FITNESS TO INDEPENDENCE

By the time you begin working this chapter you will have obtained financial fitness. I can not congratulate you enough on improving the quality of your life.

However your goal should be for continuous improvements. Always try to find ways to make your life better and happier. One way to do this is to turn financial fitness into financial independence.

There are several steps that follow fitness towards independence. These steps just like the others require research, dedication and persistent action. We will begin with the very basics.

GED

If you have never obtained your high school education or GED then that is the first thing that you need to correct. In today's marketplace there are opportunities that will never be available to you if you do not have a diploma. With all the night schools and home study courses available there is no excuse for you to be without a diploma. No matter how old you are, it is never too late to start.

I have an uncle that is over 50 years old and he just recently obtained his high school diploma. If you do not have a diploma obtain one as soon as possible.

SPECIALIZED TRAINING

If you are already high school educated the first place you will start is with specialized training. In order to make yourself more valuable in the marketplace you will need to learn how to do something that not anyone can do. The more specialized training you have, the more valuable you become, and the more money that you will inevitably make.

My dad worked in an assembly plant nearly all his life. He had some specialized training in welding with MIG and TIG welders that put him at top pay in the plant but still he wasn't a certified welder. He finally got tired of the dead-end job at the factory and obtained a CDL license to drive a truck. A lot of people tried to discourage my dad. I mean, at his age here he was going to school to become a truck driver. My dad didn't listen to the negatives, he did what he had to in order to obtain the license and learn to drive a truck. My dad now owns his own truck and makes more money than he made before in the factory.

I have an acquaintance whose wife was looking for a job. Her husband had done a favor for a local dentist and had asked the dentist to give his wife a job as a receptionist in payment for the favor. The dentist did give the lady a job.

Over the next three years or so the lady took a home study course in order to become a dental hygienist. The lady is now well on her way to becoming a dentist herself and just recently received a large bonus for an internship she had done as well an additional sign up bonus from another practice where she will work. She now makes more money than her husband who helped her get the job does.

I myself obtained a license to operate wastewater treatment plants when I got out of high school. I took some college courses and up-graded my licenses. Within a year I was making more money than most of the people that graduated at the top of my class.

After that I obtained an insurance license and a SEC license in order to work part-time in the financial services industry for extra money. I did eventually work full-time in the financial service industry but at one time I had three specialized licenses.

At present I am licensed with the U.S. Coast Guard to pilot towboats and I also have a Merchant Mariners Document that allows me to load and discharge chemicals in and out of barges. My job pays me very well and allows me three months per year of off time.

My point is not to say how wonderful I am but to impress upon you that you should gain all the specialized training that you possibly can. It will put you at the top of your game.

Now specialized training takes money. That is absolutely correct so a portion of the money that you have freed up will go to this training. We will make plans of action for the allocation of this money shortly.

Let me mention that specialized training is an on-going process. Once you have obtained knowledge in a certain field of expertise, don't stop. You always have the option to improve your life through books and tape programs that will be key in your financial independence.

BUILD AN EMERGENCY FUND

An emergency fund is a fund to compensate for the little curves that life throws you. You never know when you might lose your job or get injured, for this reason you need funds set aside to carry you through. The experts recommend and I agree that you should have six months worth of income set aside in liquid assets. Liquid assets are simply assets that are easily transferred into cash. Investments such as real estate are not liquid enough because you will have to sell property in order to obtain cash.

I will recommend three places to accumulate this money only because they are my personal favorites. I recommend that you split up your emergency fund into a money market account, a very conservative mutual fund that is not an IRA and in gold coin or bouillon.

$ _____ X 6 MONTHS = EMERGENCY FUND
(Gross monthly income)

DETERMINE RETIREMENT AMOUNT

In order to find out what you will need to do to be financially independent there are a couple of things that you can do.

The first thing that you can do is to find a company to do an analysis of your finances that will pinpoint what you need to do right now in order to retire financially independent. I very much recommend that you have one of these done.

Usually companies that sell securities will be able to help you with this service. The price of this service can run from quite expensive to free. Call the mutual fund companies and ask what the cost of this service is. Some are willing to provide this as a free service in order to obtain your business.

Next you can obtain a financial calculator, learn to use it and spend a lot of time trying to figure compound interest. That is the hard way to go.

Last you can use the charts that follow to figure compound interest. The factors on these charts are the same factors that are programmed into a financial calculator but you can use them with a common ordinary calculator.

The charts have basic instructions included on them and they will help you determine what you need to do to obtain financial independence.

LUMP SUM INVESTMENT
COMPOUND INTEREST CHART

# YEARS	6%	7%	8%	9%	10%	11%	12%
5	1.338	1.403	1.469	1.539	1.610	1.685	1.762
10	1.791	1.967	2.159	2.367	2.594	2.839	3.105
15	2.397	2.759	3.172	3.642	4.177	4.785	5.473
20	3.207	3.870	4.661	5.604	6.727	8.062	9.646
25	4.292	5.427	6.848	8.623	10.835	13.585	17.00
30	5.740	7.612	10.063	13.268	17.449	22.892	29.959

In order to find out how much a one- time investment will grow to in a specific number of years at a specific interest rate find the factor that coincides with the number of years and the interest rate and multiply the lump amount by the factor. Example to find how much $5,000 will be worth in 15 years at 9% multiply $5,000 by 3.642. The answer is $18,210.

YEARLY INVESTMENT
COMPOUND INTEREST CHART

# YEARS	6%	7%	8%	9%	10%	11%	12%
5	5.975	6.153	6.336	6.623	6.716	6.913	7.115
10	13.972	14.784	15.645	16.560	17.531	18.561	19.654
15	24.673	26.888	29.324	32.003	34.950	38.190	41.753
20	38.993	43.865	49.423	55.765	63.002	71.265	80.698
25	58.156	67.676	78.954	92.324	108.182	126.999	149.333
30	83.802	101.073	122.346	148.575	180.943	220.913	270.292

In order to find out how much a yearly investment will grow to in a specific number of years at a particular interest rate find the factor that coincides with the number of years and the interest rate and multiply the yearly amount by the factor. Example to find out how much a $2,000 per year investment will be worth in 20 years at a compound interest rate of 6%, multiply $2,000 by 38.993. The answer is $77,986.

PLAN YOUR RETIREMENT NOW

Determine the amount of money needed for retirement and make sure that you will have it when you retire. A simple rule of thumb to figure how much you will need is to decide how much per year that you want to live on and add 5% to that for each year that you have until retirement for inflation.

That is how much money you will need per year in order to retire. Take your yearly amount and divide it by 12 in order to get a monthly amount for retirement.

Next take your monthly amount and multiply it by 100. That will give you a very rough idea of how much cash you will need in order to draw the monthly amount off of a mutual fund without running out of money. However this is the time to use your compound interest charts in order to find out the exact amount and I would further recommend that you discuss this with whomever you purchased your mutual fund with. Do not guess find out exactly what you need and how much that you need to be putting up now in order to obtain your retirement goals.

LIVE ON 70% OF YOUR INCOME

Once you have a clear picture of how much you need to retire on the next step is to finance the trip from fitness to independence. In order to do this you will need to learn to live on 70% of your income. This 70% should include all the utilities that you have to pay plus any bills that you have and also finance what ever it is that you like to do in your leisure. Living off of 70% of your income should be no problem now that you have obtained financial fitness. The other 30% you will use for financial independence.

THE OTHER 30%

Give 10% of your income to a charity or organization that you feel good about. After all you are more fortunate than most to be financially fit so give something back. It is strictly my opinion but I would recommend that you give to the people closest to you. In other words don't go around the world until you have gone across town.

I think it is a shame when our government sends money and food to people in other countries when there are people starving in America. Let's take care of our own then we can help in other countries.

I am not begrudging anyone anything and if sending money overseas is what you feel strongly about then by all means do so. Like I said it is strictly my opinion.

If you feel uncomfortable with giving your money to a group or organization for this purpose because you don't really know what they do with your money then buy groceries yourself and give them to a needy family in your community.

The next 10% should be put into your emergency fund until it has reached the amount totaling your six month gross income and then invested in a mutual fund of your choosing for retirement.

The final 10% should be put towards building your wealth. It is an investment in you. This 10% will at first finance your specialized training and will be there to continue your training when you need it. On a larger scale if there is something that you like to do part time that you believe that you could turn into a profit use this 10% to fund that project.

Myself I am a songwriter and I spend a lot of time and money producing songs and sending them to Nashville in the hopes of having one on the radio some day. I am constantly buying equipment, tapes CDs and investing money in songwriting contests.

This 10% will add zest and purpose to your life. Every time that I receive a new demo in the mail of a song that I have written, I am just like a kid in a candy store.

So this is the money that you use to try to increase your income whether you invest it in real estate or in repairing and re-selling used cars. Everyone has a talent that this money can be used for and most talents can be turned into capitol. If you are unsure of your talents and what you want to do with this money then refer to your wish list for ideas.

FINANCIAL INDEPENDENCE PLAN OF ACTION:

START DATE: ___-___-___   **PLANNED COMPLETION DATE:** ___-___-___

PURPOSE: After attaining financial fitness to become financially independent and retire comfortably.

_____**STEP 1:** Learn to live off of 70% of our income.

_____**STEP 2:** Establish an emergency fund using 10% of our income in very conservative investments with a balance of at least 6 months of our gross income. After the emergency fund is established invest that 10% toward retirement.

$_____ **X 6 MONTHS = EMERGENCY FUND**
   (Gross monthly income)

_____**STEP 3:** Determine the amount we need for retirement and continue to invest 10% towards its attainment.
$_____ **PLUS 5% PER YEAR FOR**
(Amount needed per year to live on)
_____ **DIVIDED BY 12 TIMES 100 EQUALS**
(# Years until retirement)

$_____**BASIC AMOUNT NEEDED FOR RETIREMENT**

_____**STEP 4:** Give 10% back in the form of charitable donations.

_____**STEP 5:** Invest 10% of our income into specialized training and then into the creation of wealth. The income that we create will be split up 70/30 in this plan as well.

_____**STEP 6: OBTAIN FINANCIAL INDEPENDENCE**

COMPLETION DATE: _____-_____-_____

As stated through out this book, I have been on top and I have been on the bottom in my personal pursuit of financial fitness. There are forks in the road and obstacles to overcome with any journey. It takes dedication and determination to make any plan work. Nothing, however seems to go exactly as planned therefore we must learn patients and rely on our own creativity to overcome the challenges that life has to offer.

Whatever you do, don't give up. You can accomplish anything that you set your mind to do with consistent effort over a period of time. Even if it takes years to accomplish your goals you will be making continuous improvements during those years that will greatly improve your quality of life as you go.

In closing I would like to pass one final idea along to you. A winner doesn't even realize that he is in a race. A winner just shows up because he likes to run. So run toward financial fitness because you like the idea of being debt-free.

I do thank you very much for reading my book. I certainly hope that you enjoyed it and found it educational as well as easy to understand. I wish for you all the financial fitness that you deserve and I know that you will achieve success in your endeavors. This now is the end of this book but it is just the beginning for you and your future. May God bless!

THE END

SONGWRITER
BY WILLIE NELSON
FROM THE MOVIE "SONGWRITER"

WRITE IT DOWN WHAT YOU FOUND OUT...SONGWRITER
  DON'T LET IT ALL SLIP AWAY.
SPEAK YOUR MIND ALL THE TIME...SONGWRITER
  SOMEONE IS LISTENING TODAY.

SO WRITE ON...SONGWRITER
  WRITE ON SONGWRITER
WRITE ON...SONGWRITER
  WRITE ON...SONGWRITER...

For additional copies of this book please send a check or money order for $19.95 plus $3.00 shipping and handling to:

Joe Kent
P.O. Box 1205
Folsom, La. 70437

WHY NOT BE DEBT-FREE?

Are you tired of living from paycheck to paycheck and always having too much month left over at the end of the money? Wouldn't you rather have your money working for you instead of someone else? This instruction book is your complete guide for reducing debts, building wealth and living a more prosperous life. Whether you make $15,000 per year or $115,000 per year you will refer to this manual again and again.

You will discover:

$- A simple way to determine the rate at which your money will double and how to increase that rate

$- A secret that the financial institutions do not want you to know that could save you a quarter of a million dollars

$- Easy ways to reduce your tax burden

$- How to get the most amount of insurance coverage for the least amount of money and use the difference to eliminate the need for insurance all together

$- How to pay off high interest personal debt and operate on a cash-only basis

$- How to improve your credit in 4 months

$- How to cut years off of a 30 year mortgage and save thousands of dollars in interest

$- How to develop your own FINANCIAL FITNESS plan and what you need to do now to become financially independent

$- How to determine where your money actually goes

$- A fast and easy way to balance your checking account

FINANCIAL FITNESS
THE INSTRUCTION BOOK FOR YOUR PAYCHECK

JOIN THE HUNDREDS OF SUCCESSFUL PEOPLE WHO HAVE TAKEN CONTROL OF THEIR FINANCIAL DESTINIES!

Are you tired of living from paycheck to paycheck and always having too much month left over at the end of the money? Have you tried to get ahead financially and failed? Now at last for those who seriously want to become debt-free and live a more prosperous life there is a guaranteed way. It is called FINANCIAL FITNESS. This incredible book is complete from "A" to "Z". It is easy to read and understand and explains everything that you need to know-step-by-step to gain control of your financial future.

THE AMERICAN DREAM

We live in one of the richest countries in the world yet almost 90% of the people that retire every year do so on an income considered to be at the poverty level. For most people financial independence seems like a dream that will never come true and operating on a cash only basis is out of the question. However it is possible. There are lots of common people who have succeeded financially with no formal education or special talents. One thing these people had in common was the utilization of one or all of the secrets that are revealed in this amazing book.

NO SCHEMES

None of the secrets revealed in FINANCIAL FITNESS are get-rich-quick-schemes. They are however basic techniques that will lead you to the financial future that everyone wants for their family. If you have ever dreamed of being debt-free and living a prosperous life then this book is for you.

START NOW

This incredible book gives you step-by-step instructions on how to build wealth while reducing liabilities. Every detail has been covered so that you can tailor the secrets to your own personal situation. Whether you make $15,000 per year or $115,000, you will refer to this manual again and again. Every secret is proven to produce results in your financial future. They have made and saved thousands of dollars for hundreds of people. Now for the first time ever, all of the secrets have been revealed in this fascinating book. So place your order Now! Don't wait to get in on this powerful opportunity. Simply fill in the handy order form, enclose check or money order and mail it TODAY!

YOU WILL DISCOVER

$-A simple way to determine the rate at which your savings will double and how to increase that rate
$-A secret that financial institutions don't want you to know that could be worth a quarter of a million-dollars to you
$-How to pay off high interest debt and live on cash instead of credit
$-How to drastically improve your credit in 4 months
$-How to cut years off of your mortgage and save thousands in interest
$-What you need to do now to become financially independent-and much more

GUARANTEE

Order FINANCIAL FITNESS now. If you are not satisfied return it within 10 days for a full refund. No questions asked. That is our guarantee.

Please rush my copy of FINANCIAL FITNESS. I've enclosed $19.95 + $3.00 S/H
__Check __Money Order made payable to Joe Kent

NAME_____

ADDRESS_____

CITY_____STATE_____ZIP_____

Send to Joe Kent   P.O. Box 1205, Folsom, La. 70437